The Technique
of Inner Action

The Technique
of Inner Action

The Soul of a Performer's Work

Bill Bruehl

HEINEMANN
Portsmouth, NH

Heinemann
A division of Reed Elsevier Inc.
361 Hanover Street
Portsmouth, NH 03801-3912
Offices and agents throughout the world

Every effort has been made to contact the copyright holders and students for
permission to reprint borrowed material. We regret any oversights that may
have occurred and would be happy to rectify them in future printings of this
work.

Acquisitions Editor: Lisa Barnett
Production Editor: Renée M. Nicholls
Cover Designer: Tom Allen/Pear Graphic Design
Author Photo: David Cross

Library of Congress Cataloging-in-Publication Data

Bruehl, Bill.
    The technique of inner action : the soul of a performer's work /
Bill Bruehl.
        p. cm.
    Includes bibliographical references.
    ISBN 0-435-08687-1 (alk. paper)
    1. Acting. 2. Method (Acting) I. Title.
PN2061.B78   1995
792'.028--dc20   95-16495
                                                                        CIP

Printed in the United States of America on acid-free paper
99 98 97 96   DA   1 2 3 4 5

For My Three Angels:
Margaret Ellen Bruehl-Gauger
Amelia Susan Kroes-Bruehl
and
Alexandra Brunato-Bruehl

Contents

Acknowledgments

*T*his little book gestated in me for more than twenty years. My primary concern as an actor, director, and teacher has always been authenticity of expression. Though I'd read Stanislavski almost from the beginning of my career, the fact that authenticity was also his primary concern and that he had essentially solved the problem toward the end of his life dawned slowly. As a result, I spend my years at Stony Brook University experimenting with and developing my own technique for the expression of authenticity in performance with students in both scene study classes and improvisation workshops. They that were both students and subjects was something I was hardly aware of at first, though I think many of them realized it by watching me grapple with problems that arose in our work together. The insights in this book about the difference between the actor's personal objectives and the objectives of the character in the script emerged from work with the Stony Brook theatre students. The applicability of these insights to all kinds of public performance emerged from my work with medical and pre-law students, and with teachers.

But this was a slippery matter to clarify in concrete prose. How does one make clear such ambiguous concepts as taking a risk and total self-acceptance? How can one make concrete on the written page the idea that spontaneity occurs in the context of a thoroughly rehearsed performance? For years, it seemed that the only way to disseminate these ideas about authenticity was in an improvisation workshop or class.

Over time, however, I also found myself applying the ideas in rehearsals while directing, and applying entirely new rehearsal methods for work about to be performed. Gradually, because of the willingness of actors to take risks and test my ideas in rehearsals and performances, I began to see how this book could be written. I wish I had the space to name all those students and actors, but they know who they are. I thank them because it was their willingness to risk that made this little book possible.

There are others to whom I am also indebted, especially Terry Schreiber, who urged me to stop talking and do it when we were having lunch in a Second Avenue coffee shop four years ago. Colleagues like Rose Zimbardo, John Cameron, Amy Sullivan, and Farley Richmond at Stony Brook also encouraged the project. John and Amy even made themselves vulnerable by participating in some of the workshops. Amy has begun to apply these ideas to her own work as a choreographer. Fellow playwrights Mary Duncan-Steidl, Steven Daedalus Burch, and Angelo Parra challenged me, urged me on, and made significant contributions. And, just as she has for forty years, it is my wife, Margaret, who always grabs the tiller and steers me through dark days when doubts rage.

Lisa Barnett, my editor at Heinemann, is the person who made the most profound impact on the final development of the manuscript. It was her humor, wit, enthusiasm, confidence, and her willingness to challenge, along with her patience with my foibles, that finally made all the difference.

Introduction

The premise of this book is that the fundamental task for an actor preparing a piece for performance is to find and articulate the inner actions or objectives of the character. The ensuing flow of these inner actions defines the character externally for the audience. Mastery of the technique of inner action leads to the ability to control those complex forces of expression that bring magic to performance. And controlling that magic enables performers to bring uniqueness and excitement into live performances as dependably as the stage magician can create believable illusions.

In fact, the technique of inner action brings craftsmanship to the soul of performance and allows the performer to consistently engage and convince the audience that it is experiencing emotional truth. Some actors misuse the technique; some find it difficult to master. But discerning the inner actions of characters gives actors a tool to ensure the best use of native talents and creative possibilities.

This book is not written for actors alone, although it is written to them. The technique of inner action is relevant to every style of theatre, Eastern or Western. It is useful for singers, dancers, public speakers, and actors on stage or in film. And knowing how the process of inner action works and what it can lead to will help producers, directors, writers, critics, and anyone else wanting to better understand the mysteries of performance.

To begin, I'd like to invite you to participate in an easy, experiential exercise by following the directions below. Doing the exercise should make my basic thesis much clearer.

First, look at your right hand palm up. Focus on the first joint of your ring finger. Now decide that, no matter what, you will move that top joint and nothing else on that hand. Your *inner action* is to wiggle only that first joint. Do not allow any other movement to occur anywhere else in that hand. Is it hard to do? Try again. Just hold out your hand palm up and make sure nothing else moves while you wiggle that top joint. No success yet? You are dealing with obstacles and you are involved in a dramatic action. *Nothing moved, and you have been in action.* Movement, contrary to popular opinion, is not a prerequisite for action.

When I try this exercise with my students and colleagues, there is usually no external movement beyond the quiver of nervous tension. You want to move only the top joint of your ring finger but other joints and digits want to move, too! The physical structure of your hand restricts the free movement of only that ring finger top joint. Often I see that fatigue sets in as my students (and perhaps you) continue to struggle, still involved in inner action, in drama. Your drama, your action. The point in doing the exercise is that this "action" has (probably) not resulted in the desired external movement! All of the action has been within you, unseen by the world. It has been *inner action*. In fact, this drama has consisted entirely of action within one person. Observers would have seen only a person quietly looking at an unmoving hand, apparently struggling with some kind of frustrated inner need.

Now try another tactic through putting some *activity* into the action. Bring in some help by holding your right hand with your left. (I never said you couldn't use your other hand). Now try. If you have to, hold all the other fingers until you can finally move that top joint and nothing else. In other words, in your struggle to execute your inner action, you have changed tactics; you have employed other—subsidiary—"inner actions." Maybe you decided *to cheat* or *to make it happen any way you can* or *to outsmart me*. These are all secondary inner actions in pursuit of moving your top joint—your primary inner action—that evoke a variety of external activities to help you achieve your aspiration.[1] This book is about all of these kinds of inner actions. Mastery of the craft of inner actions enables the performer to achieve consistent, authentic, and magical expression, which is the true aim of all performance.

I do not discuss the external technique of the actor in this book because external technique has been widely discussed and accepted. Unfortunately, this level of acceptance may be too extreme; there is a general perception that the craft of acting is an external craft. While I hope to change that perception, there is no argument in this book about the value of external training. I highly value the mastery of physical skills such as vocal technique. The technique of inner action, however, is the equal and necessary complement of external technique. The relationship must be well balanced, for external technique without effective inner work risks becoming pretense.[2]

The work of singers and musicians, teachers and lawyers, sales clerks and dancers, politicians and ministers, and professional and amateur performers from all of the world's performance traditions will turn from the mechanical to the magical with a proper understanding of inner action and its relationship to external activities. Even fans will develop a deeper level of appreciation for the performer's work after understanding the kinds of inner action guiding the performances they watch and critique. Although I will focus on the stage actor, I expect that readers whose interest lies in many other areas will find making the translation easy and instantaneous.

*Commanding, entreating,
relating, menacing,
interrogating, answering . . .
belong . . . to the art of acting.*

—*Aristotle*, The Poetics

The Meaning and Role of Inner Action

1

Categories of Inner Action: Poison and Magic

*I*n the introduction, I tried to demonstrate inner "action" in contrast to external "activity." But understanding inner action is not easy, and applying it appropriately to a performance may be quite challenging. I recently worked with a friend who is a classically trained Bharatanatyam dancer. Her performances are supposed to be excitingly sensual and supple but had become formal and distant though quite correct. When we began to work on the inner actions of one of her characters, a palpable change instantly occurred. The dancer's entire being lightened, and brightened with a sexy electricity. Why? Because she had begun *to woo* Krishna, the object of her desire, instead of trying *to perform* the gestures correctly or *to please* her teacher, which had become unconscious inner actions. As an unforeseen consequence of years of training that concentrated on externals, the pressure to do everything "correctly" had displaced her focus on her character's inner actions. Thus, there are two kinds of inner action; one is poison to the actor, and one leads to performance magic. The latter kind of inner action mobilizes the actor's performance of the character. But the former kind flows from the performer's personal inner needs.

It is essential that we realize that these two categories of inner action exist. We must understand that the only appropriate inner actions to take into performance are those that the *characters* are struggling to achieve. The actor has a responsibility to discover those other inner actions—often unconscious—that apply only to the actor's private life and to separate them from character actions. Apart from an exception that I will get into later, the actor must strive to not bring personal inner actions into performance, even unconsciously.

Consider Oedipus in *Oedipus Rex.* The play begins with the people of Thebes pleading with him to save their city from a ravaging plague of death and decay. He tells them that the health and happiness of the people are all he cares about and that he would do anything to stop the plague. He is told the plague will abate only after the murderer of their former King Laius is found. Oedipus promises to do everything he can to find the killer. Is that Oedipus's primary objective, his most important inner action? Maybe.

The first task of the actor preparing the part of Oedipus is to discover the primary inner action, the action that Stanislavski called the superobjective. And is finding the killer the superobjective Oedipus agrees to carry out? Or is it *to drive* the killer out of the city? Or *to please* his people, *to enhance* his own power, or something else? My method of identifying the superobjectives is to ask why this character would carry out these actions. Why does he want to find the killer? *To cleanse* the city of the plague. Why does he want to drive him away? By so doing he will *purify* the city. What about *loving* or *pleasing* his people? These are unlikely objectives. He already loves his people and he pleases them with his very being. Nor does he wish to enhance his power. We learn from the chorus that he has all the power there is to have. His people regard him as a godlike savior.

What, then, is his primary, overarching struggle? Let us assume here that Oedipus wants *to cleanse* the city. That is a character action, something the character will attempt to achieve. But let's suppose that the *actor* playing Oedipus, consciously or unconsciously, wants *to ingratiate* himself with his audience. Suppose he wants *to please* his audience and brings that "action" into his performance. His interpretation of Oedipus's words will not make any sense. We have already seen that his people are pleased by his very being, that there is no interest in pleasing, and if the actor wants to please there will be a chasm between the actor's behavior and the words he speaks. Oedipus's actions have nothing to do with pleasing anybody.

I believe that apart from external ineptitude, most bad acting arises from the performer's confusion of the actor's and the character's inner action. Actors and directors and teachers must become aware of the possibility of this confusion. Once aware of the potential, it is easy for actors to see that they are playing the wrong actions. The last thing in the world Oedipus wants to do is *to please* his director or *to look good* for his audience. Oedipus doesn't give a damn about pleasing or looking good. He will *purge* at any price. His determination to do so is part of his tragedy. And until the actor is aware of the inner actions he is playing he hasn't learned to incarnate Oedipus. Yes, he may know the lines, speak with clarity, and walk with grace, but his performance is dead or boring. If he substitutes his personal inner actions for the inner actions of the character, he will poison his performance.

When I see a pretentious, inert, or confusing performance, my first guess is that the actor and the director have not clarified the character's inner actions, and I suspect that the actor is more concerned with personal than character aspirations. Maybe the actor wants to look good on stage or stand tall. Maybe the actor wants *to be* something instead of going after the things that Oedipus wants to do.

Most actors' personal inner actions are concerned with getting, pleasing, making, doing, and being. These are not the specific, animated, concrete verbs that define character. Oedipus wants *to purify* the city. We do not want to sit in the audience and watch him trying *to please* or *to obey*. Such a performance would make no sense. Though it may be externally correct, it will have none of the inner truth that is the source of the performer's magic—an inner truth that arises from inner action.

If for no other reason, a performer should understand the technique of inner action to avoid this potential confusion between personal and character inner actions. Every performer must learn that these two categories of inner action exist and distinguish between them. We have to find, clarify, and articulate the inner actions of the character in the script and separate those intentions from personal aspirations. We make our acting problems especially troublesome when we fail to articulate our character's actions, when we go on stage unfocused and susceptible to personal motives, especially those that have to do with doing good work.

What Is Inner Action?

To act is to pursue an inner action that the character wants to achieve. Petruchio wants *to win* Katherine in *The Taming of the Shrew.* If you tried the finger exercise, you wanted *to move* a recalcitrant finger joint. That was your action even if there was no external movement. It is important to keep in mind that I am not talking about external movement but action inside you. *Action,* in the dramatic sense I am using the word, is purely internal and may or may not be accompanied by any external *activity.* You could have been utterly still, even literally paralyzed, when you pursued the action to move that joint. If you did pursue the action, you were acting. You were acting because in the most fundamental sense to act is to pursue an inner action regardless of external activity.

To act is to pursue an action. It is impossible to repeat this simple but elusive fact too often. The word actor ultimately comes from the Greek *agein,* meaning to do, drive, or lead. The actor is the pursuer of action. Yet we seem not to notice that to act is to pursue an action, thinking instead that actors try to be somebody. Actors do not, should not, and must not ever try to "be." They play with action. Actors are occasionally listed on performance programs as "The Players," and the German word for actor is *Spieler,* literally "player." Actors play, and playing is a certain kind of action. Performing is not about "being." Actors act, dancers dance, singers sing.

And although a performer's work is described with active verbs, we continually seem to confuse the work of performers as being rather than action. To develop a craft for performance, we have to forget anything we may have heard or believed about actors trying *to be* somebody. That concept is the perception of an untutored audience. The audience sees the result and confuses result with process. Actors must understand their own process, and the reality is that no actor, despite any individual genius, should ever try *to be* anyone other than him or herself. It is impossible. The only person I can be is me. I can't be Trigorin in *The Seagull.* It is a logical impossibility because the person Trigorin doesn't exist. I don't become Trigorin except as an illusion that I have created for the audience. What I might hope to do is to pair some of those characteristics that are mine with the *"character"*-istics that Chekhov has gathered together to define Trigorin. The result is an incarnation, a giving of flesh—my flesh—to an idea on paper. Because all we know about Trigorin is Chekhov's code for the creation of the character, the playwright and I will create this Trigorin together, applying the inner actions found in the given circumstances of Chekhov's script.

From the perspective of craft it is misleading for an actor to think of being Lady Macbeth in *Macbeth*. Instead, an actor can only understand her background and what she wants to do and then to find, articulate, and execute the actions that define the character—like making herself queen—that Lady Macbeth will fight to achieve. The actor who thinks she can be Lady Macbeth by trying *to be* cruel or wily or manipulative or loony will only suc-ceed in indicating and stereotyping those states of being.

The essential first step for performers is to eliminate from the mind the idea that skilled actors spend their time trying to be somebody other than themselves. We have to remember that at a fundamental level performance is about working with inner action. Obviously, the skilled actor will be concerned with the way she wants her character to carry herself. She must take care with the way her character speaks and with makeup, hair, and costume. But these matters, as important as they are, are all sec-ondary to the primary and fundamental matter of finding, articu-lating, and performing the flow of her character's actions. All of the external traits of the character are best used when they enhance or illuminate a character's inner actions. Falstaff's traits signal his choices of action. He is fat because he chooses to overeat, to indulge. A character should look the way he does because of choices of inner action that are inherent in the play. Performers have to forget trying to be somebody and concern themselves with the actions that define character.

Not only should the actor not go on stage trying to be some-body else, she shouldn't go on stage worrying about being angry or loving or confused or any of the other complex emotional states we are heir to. Katherine in *The Taming of the Shrew* strug-gles not to be angry or bitchy but to put fools in their place. Feeling is a state of being, and actors do not go on stage *to feel* or *be* any kind of internal state. Characters are created with a need *to do* something.

The audience's perspective is often different and we should not confuse it with ours. To the audience member the successful actor has become somebody—which after all is the objective of the art! She has become Lady Macbeth. Good. So the audience thinks the actor has *tried to be* that which she has become. Wrong. The skillful actor has not tried to do that. That transformation is an illusion, magician's work, and it doesn't help the actor to think as the audience does. The actor has to think about the actions she must work with to create the illusion for the audience. Only the skilled performer who works with carefully articulated and rehearsed inner actions can be sure consistently to create that transformation. The actor will mislead or deceive herself by saying that she wants to be Lady Macbeth. That is the thinking of a person without a reflective inner technique.

We will go into the history of this matter in a later chapter, but I'd like to take a moment and point out a fact of theater history. Until Stanislavski, critical theories about the actor's inner workings almost always proceeded from an audience point of view that focuses on how well actors express feelings. For centuries critics and fans watching the actor work have wondered how actors can express feelings on stage night after night in such an exciting and convincing way. Their discussions always and understandably concentrated on the psychology of emotion itself. How do we as actors feel? What do we feel? What is feeling? Can actors fool the audience? Do actors perform only the physical signs of feeling? It is only in our time that we have come to see that authentic emotional expression is an automatic function of the actor having taken into himself the struggles of the character. We will begin to have a truly sophisticated discussion about performance when critics and audiences set aside their concern with feelings and focus on the flow of inner actions.

The skillful actor's approach to her work is more like, "What do I need to know and do in order to make them accept the illusion that I have become Norma Desmond, or Lady Macbeth, or Madame Arkadina?" The answer is that the actor must know everything she can know about her character's background. She must rationally decide and name the changing feeling states of her character from moment to moment even though she does not go on stage to execute feeling states like ennui, despair, boredom, happiness, or anger. She goes on stage determined to execute the actions that drive the character, those unseen inner actions that are like your trying to move your finger joint.

In addition to learning all she can about the character—including feeling states—the skilled actor also knows she has to identify and articulate and master the flow of the character's inner actions. If she pursues those inner actions with passion in her performance, she can work knowing that the emotional expression will happen automatically and authentically. Know the given circumstances and struggle for your action (or intention/objective) and the expression of genuine feeling will happen automatically. This is a point of major importance, first articulated by Stanislavski.

The skilled actor preparing Lady Macbeth does not go on stage saying, "I want to go on stage motivated to do anger." Yes, she does have to come to know in a rational and analytical way that her character is angry at some given moment, but she does not come on to enact anger. Though we see a distressed woman trying to clean the blood off her hands, the actress may be trying *to obliterate* her sins; frustrated, she will begin to feel a complex mix of frustration, anger, dismay, sadness, fear, and all of the other feelings that might exist in the complex human moment that Shakespeare created.

In contrast, I can't think of any "character" who wants to enact an emotion. Theoretically, though, there may be some. Perhaps Jill wants to win Jack and thinks that weeping may be the way to do it. If so, the actor playing Jill is really playing out the action *to win* by using a tactic *to gain* pity or *to provoke* guilt. The actor playing Stanley in Williams's *A Streetcar Named Desire* should never choose to enact anger. Stanley doesn't want to act out anger and to try to do so could produce a childish and temperamental Stanley. The audience would sense an incongruity because the script isn't written that way. What Stanley probably wants is *to intimidate* or *to dominate*, actions that may evoke anger and other complex emotional states.

Trying to enact emotions encourages stereotyping, pretension, falseness, and bombast—states that indicate or show the idea of an emotion. The actor trying to enact emotion is trying to do something (trying to feel or be) that doesn't fit the actions of the character as written. Hamlet is not trying *to be* or not *be* and he isn't trying *to be* confused. He is *puzzling* out a conundrum in the "To be or not to be" speech. That struggle *to puzzle* will automatically cause the actor to feel the cluster of emotion that is "confusion" or "contemplation." He will then express that authentic feeling state spontaneously using his entire being.

Think about it for a moment from your own perspective. Try *to be* angry and confused. Take a moment and do it. *Be* angry and confused. I don't know about you, but I just blank out. It is an idea that doesn't compute. It doesn't confuse or baffle me to try *to be* confused. The effort just takes me nowhere. It is not part of my rational processes. It stops action.

If the objective of the actor playing Hamlet is *to feel*, he would give a bad performance for two reasons. First, Hamlet is not trying "to feel." He is not paralyzed, brain dead, or stuporous. He is actively trying *to avenge* his father's murder, which is why at the moment of the monologue he is puzzling out his condition. *To feel* would produce an entirely wrong kind of Hamlet. In the second place, trying to enact a feeling state has the tendency to lead actors to portray the stereotypical idea of what a feeling looks like. Since ideas are not feelings, enacting a stereotypical idea of an emotion leads to a false, and deadly performance. Actors call this "playing a mood," and it leads to the actor's worst sin: indicating. To indicate feeling results in bad acting and yet, astonishingly, we still see audiences applaud it.

I suggest that one reason we accept canned goods on stage is that our culture believes that actors are gifted, shamanlike creatures. We think they don't really know how they do what they do, that we mustn't disturb the trance because maybe it'll be better next time. Because of the neglect of the technique of inner action, even some theater people believe that actors have no craft for evoking the authentic inner self. The myth that all of this is a divine mystery and that as a result we mustn't be too demanding lives on professionally even today.

This attitude might be valid when we go to see our kids perform in the fourth-grade orchestra, but we have to hold all actors, including community amateurs, to a higher standard. We do that for other craftspeople. We demand that woodworkers consistently make their tables stand square and strong and level. Actors should meet the same standard of consistency. They should engage us emotionally and without distraction from the beginning to the final curtain. And every actor I know wants audiences to demand that standard as a minimum.

Anything else demeans both our actors and our theater. We have a craft that enables the actor to master his inner workings. The craft is not mysterious and we have had it available for most of this century. Of course, fifty or seventy-five years may not have been time enough. And we still have history to contend with. After all, for most of human history actors expressed authentic emotional states without knowing how to work consciously with inner action. There are still many intuitive performers working today, people who are willing to say that what they do is a mystery, that they've never articulated what they are actually doing on stage. "I don't know. I say the lines, go where and when I'm told, and it happens." Right. Sometimes they produce magic, too. Sometimes.

What are the consequences of the intuitive approach? Uncertainty, for one thing. Actors who work intuitively do not have the craft to know why their performance was so wonderful last night and fell flat tonight. They do not know why it fell flat because they have not articulated for themselves what their character is struggling for. Another consequence is that the first intuitive choice that actors may be tempted to make tends to be commonplace or predictable. Easy choices do not stimulate the creative imagination. As we'll see in a later chapter, the technique of inner action is a creative process that can help the actor probe creative possibilities in rehearsal. Directors who employ the technique of inner action in rehearsals never plague their actors with the boredom of mindless repetition.

Nevertheless, there is resistance to the technique of inner action, to finding the right verbs and articulating them. Stanislavski noted this resistance among the actors he worked with. It is a resistance that causes some acting teachers to give up on this approach. While some directors use it, many do not. I suspect that part of the source of this resistance is the difficulty in finding the words. What does Willie Loman want to do in Miller's *Death of a Salesman?* There is no quick and easy answer, but perhaps the brilliant, intuitive actor might just know what Willie wants to achieve. His problem will be that until he somehow articulates Willie's intention, the actor will lack control of that intuitive knowledge. Lacking that control he will find it difficult to say with certainty why the performance worked last night and failed tonight. Only the actor who can articulate and apply the character's inner actions can claim mastery of the craft. It is only in motion pictures that persons who haven't mastered the technique of inner action might find success. They can work for directors willing to shoot scenes repeatedly until something emerges that works or that the editor can transmute. On stage, something that works must emerge every night.

To most experienced theater professionals, this talk of inner action is old news. Stanislavski began talking about what I call inner action in the early part of the century. He used the term *objectives.* Others speak of *intentions.* Near the end of his life in the late 1930s, Stanislavski came to see that a technique of inner action is central to the actor's work. In English we call it the method of physical action. Since then, the power of Stanislavski's insight has been validated in print by masters of twentieth-century theater with widely varied styles, including people like Bertolt Brecht, Jerzy Grotowsky, Michel St. Denis, John Barton, and even Lee Strasberg.

The Right and Wrong Kinds of Inner Action

While some masters of Western theater may have recognized the value of Stanislavski's insight, few in the rest of the world have seen its relevance. I want to emphasize that the technique of inner action is applicable to every style and every genre of performance whether from the West or Asia or any other place in the world. And when I use the word *performance* I also include dance, opera, and ballet. The technique even applies to singers, stand-up comics, lawyers, and public speakers.

One reason so many have discounted the Stanislavski heritage is the persistent canard that the whole "Stanislavski System" is training for realism or naturalism. Stanislavski was aware of this wholly undeserved reputation and tried with productions at the Moscow Art Theater and in studio experiments to demonstrate that his work was not limited to these styles.

The world must come to recognize that the most important thing about his emphasis on the centrality of articulating inner actions is its applicability to every theatrical form. There is no qualification: every form. Articulating inner action is as useful to the singer or dancer as it is to the Kabuki actor or the Bharatanatyam dancer. If a singer who has always seemed technically correct but lifeless works with inner actions, his work will be transformed, filled with a new vitality and emotional life without lowering the musical standards in any way.

It is impossible to perform without an inner action. "No," the critics say, "No! It can't be! Brecht and Grotowsky? Noh theater, Beijing opera, Balanchine? No! You can't mean to say that Stanislavski is of any use to any of these!" The technique of the inner action based on the circumstances of the script or its analogue will apply to all of these. It is not an aesthetic that belongs to a specific class of performers.

To put it another way, every performer goes onto the stage with a conscious or unconscious inner action guiding her in her work. But to bring their work to the level of craft, performers must consciously articulate and work with inner action during rehearsal. Otherwise, they will never be certain they are in command of their work. The mystery of why last night's magic went dead tonight will end when you allow the technique of inner action to guide your work.

Consider the temple dancers of South Asia, such as the Bharatanatyam dancer I mentioned earlier. To the uninitiated westerner, there is probably no other type of performance more abstract. Yet every gesture means something concrete and specific to tell a story. Classical Indian dance teachers press their students to get those gestures absolutely right. The interaction of teacher and student emphasizes mechanics. The teacher conditions the student to a concern for mechanical and external perfection.

Earlier I described the experience of my friend, the professional Bharatanatyam dancer, trained according to traditional Indian norms in India. Hira Panth is also a director and dramaturg with an MFA in theater. When I first approached her with the notion that Stanislavski's ideas about acting could be applicable to South Indian classical dance, her response was a tolerant smile. It was the kind of smile you might give a brash adolescent. But my friend is a person with the grace to listen with an open mind to see if there is any connection, however slight, that might save me from embarrassment.

We explored the problem together—Hira listening to my questions about her characters and what they struggled for. We did not violate or modify any of her physical technique. What Hira found transformed her work, which was already a marvel of grace and beauty, into something immediately accessible and moving for Western audiences naive in the traditions of classic Indian forms.

In her demonstration performances, she first danced as she had always done. Then, without changing a beat or a gesture, she danced the same piece after having articulated for herself the character's inner actions. The impact on the audiences was astonishing. The work moved from being mechanically correct and merely graceful to a coy, feminine, sunny wooing that electrified her audience without modifying a gesture. Now convinced that Stanislavski's insight could powerfully impact her work, Hira went on to research whether or not India's *Bharata Natysastra,* the oldest of all performing arts treatises, echoed these twentieth-century Western ideas about inner action. It is clear from her reading that the ancient theorists were aware of the importance of inner action. In Hira's words, "Bharatha wanted to give meaning to the outer physical actions [the activities] through the inner psychological state of the mind."[3]

Like Hira Panth, Supriya Chakravarty is a traditionally trained professional. A Kathak dancer, Supriya is a practitioner of another of India's ancient classic dance-drama forms. She is an artist with a long list of credits including performances on All-India Television. A dancer of exceptional grace, elegance, and discipline, Supriya was also initially skeptical that the technique of inner action might be applicable to Kathak. However, after some discussion she thought it might affect her work and agreed to experiment. The next time I saw her she was ready to do a demonstration performance before an audience of sophisticated Western professionals. Not only that, she was even willing to let them call out surprise inner actions for her to improvise into her performance on the spot! The experiment worked, encouraging her spontaneous and appropriate emotional expression. Most of all, inner action made her work more accessible for an audience with no special knowledge of her material or traditions.

Much more research needs to be done with the technique of inner actions in all performance forms. I am sure it will benefit opera singers who have not yet found it. I have seen it favorably affect the work of young jazz and modern dancers who want to take their work beyond the bounds of technical precision. The fact is that there are many performers—dancers and singers—who know and use the technique, but as far as I can tell its application is spotty. My hope is to see it applied in all performance forms.

Even Beijing opera? Why not? The film *Farewell My Concubine* portrays students of the old Beijing opera submitting to violent beatings aimed at correcting their errors but getting no training in the actor's internal work. True, classical Chinese opera might seem more unlike Western forms than any other kind of theater, but the basic dramatic circumstances are still in play: a central character faces difficulties trying to get that to which he aspires. How about Noh? True, ideas about inner action may not be in Ze-Ami or part of that long tradition, but what would happen if contemporary Noh actors were to experiment with them? Could inner action bring a new vitality into a form that most Japanese consider to be frozen in time?

Over the last thirty years Western performance theorists and experimenters like Grotowsky have turned to Asian traditions for fresh theatrical ideas to enliven Western theater. Interest in Asian forms has grown steadily in American universities since the mid-

1960s. People are looking at the work of artists like Suzuki to find uses for the tightly disciplined and imaginative Asian approaches in our theater. Nevertheless, when I ask Asian theater scholars if Stanislavski's ideas have influenced those traditions in any way, the answer is always no. The assumption is that his work has nothing to offer classic Asian forms. Properly understood, Stanislavski's insight about inner action has the potential for reinvigorating ancient theatrical genres.

Presumably, actors like David Garrick in the eighteenth century or Henry Irving in the nineteenth, who had only experience and intuition as guides, managed to thrill and convince audiences without using any explicit theory of conscious inner technique. But if the testimony of history is valid, these types of actors have always been few. I have seen enough of the effects of Stanislavski's ideas on exotic theater forms to persuade me that the technique of inner action can deepen the emotional impact and vibrancy of any work everywhere. The technique of the inner action takes the performer beyond personal anxieties about teachers, directors, and even issues of self-worth to self-confidence and authority in all traditions.

The Superobjective, Tactics, and Other Subtleties

Until now I've focused on only one aspect of a character's inner action, what Stanislavski called the superobjective. The superobjective is the one action that characters in a drama pursue from the moment they realize what they want to accomplish until the dramatic action ends. Lady Macbeth struggles to make herself queen. Did she achieve what she struggled to accomplish? Was she able to overcome the obstacles to her struggle or not? How was her struggle or issue resolved? These are basic questions of classic dramatic structure. They always focus on the protagonist's superobjective and its resolution. But dealing with the resolution of the superobjective isn't the end of the story of inner action.

There is a continual flow of subsidiary inner actions that propel our concern about the resolution of the superobjective. The playwright maintains audience interest by creating obstacles or antagonists that block the struggle of the protagonist. Will he win? He must try another way. Will Juliet lose her man? Will Lady Macbeth win power or will the obstacles overcome or defeat her? When confronted by an obstacle the protagonist takes another tack, tries a secondary action allowing us to hope that this will open the way to the superobjective. The secondary actions or tactics create a constant flow of action. Petruchio decides that he will win Katherine. She blocks him. He tries *to woo*, but this is no good. He tries *to dominate*, but that doesn't work. He kidnaps her.

Let us agree that Hamlet's superobjective is *to avenge* his father's murder. That overarching superobjective or inner action holds our interest until the end of the play when Hamlet kills the murderer. But it is not Hamlet's only inner action. Along the way the actor playing Hamlet follows a stream of inner actions, shifting and choosing new actions as each obstacle arises. I like to think of these subsidiary actions as "tactics" that help him to achieve his main strategy: *to avenge*. Some call these changing inner actions *subobjectives,* a term that neatly describes their relationship to the superobjective.

An interesting thing about the universality of basic dramatic structure is that the actor will find the superobjective and this flow of ever changing action in the dramatic forms of every culture. Oedipus, in the theater of ancient Athens, might overcome one obstacle to his superobjective of purging the city by dominating. To deal with the next obstacle he might have *to appeal* to the gods. The next time he might have *to charge* blindly ahead. The forty-seven samurai in the Kabuki play *Chushingura* struggle using many different tactics against one obstacle after another *to avenge* their lord's death. The Bharatanatyam dancer's milkmaid wants *to woo* Krishna and tries several tactics to achieve her purpose. The generals and heroines of Beijing opera each have a flow of inner action. Hollywood moviemakers structure their characters the same way. In all these forms we will find the flow of inner actions; it is a basic part of human understanding. We want to achieve something and we change our tactics until we get it or we meet defeat. The roots of drama are in our genes.

Every dramatic character exists in a flow of these tactics or superobjectives. The entire five acts of Hamlet are driven by his superobjective. Each act has its own subobjective. Each scene in each act has its own subobjective. Each section (or beat) of each scene has its subobjective, and on the most microlevel, each moment of each beat has its own subobjective. Together this movement of objectives constitutes the flow of inner action. The skilled playwright creates this flow, and the skilled performer, aware of the flow, masters it. The would-be actor, tempted by intuition, too often capitulates into thinking that mastering that flow is too intimidating and leaves performance to chance. I discuss in a later section how an actor identifies and masters the stream of action.

The Difference Between Inner Action and External Activity

Shoot outs, sexy bed scenes, chases, explosions, or spectacular technology do not define dramatic action. Neither is it blocking—the movement around the stage. Running, laughing, and kissing are not dramatic action. It isn't behavior. The purpose of behavior—the purpose of any activity on stage—is to express inner action. When the actor playing a cop chases, arrests, and interrogates a criminal, the cop is performing *activities*. These activities are the external manifestation of inner action. In the case of the cop, the superobjective was probably to bring the criminal to justice. To execute that action our actor performed the activities of chasing, arresting, and interrogating.

Perhaps, however, the objective was really *to bring* the bad guy to justice. Or maybe she wanted *to destroy* the criminal. If she did, her activities would not be the same. She might pistol-whip, kick, or punch because the inner action *to destroy* is so different from the inner action *to bring* to justice. Articulating different inner actions can result in radically different behavior. Maybe our hypothetical cop really wants *to protect* this scoundrel by bringing him in before other criminals get to him first, leading her to do her chasing, arresting, and interrogating in a way completely unlike the other possibilities.

The most interesting fact is that a completely different complex of emotional expressions will automatically accompany each of those vastly different patterns of behavioral activity. Making a conscious choice of inner action based on an investigation of the "given circumstances" of the script determines how the actor will execute the action. That choice will decide the meaning of the playwright's words. The interpretation of a playwright's work arises from the inner actions the director and actor choose.

I want to emphasize this most important point: *The actor gives meaning to words by his choice of inner actions.* Our police officer's words "I'll get him" mean nothing alone and out of context. This simple fact gives the actor enormous power over the work of the playwright. All of the actors I know recognize the professional responsibility to respect the script, to change nothing. I am not sure that every actor realizes that actors give meaning to words. Directors and playwrights can only hope to control that process. Only by analyzing the given circumstances of the play and choosing inner actions compatible with those circumstances can the actor hope to honor the playwright's intention, and this is a wispy hope at best. The "intentional fallacy" is an old principle in literary criticism; you can't read the writer's mind to know what was intended. While we cannot consult with the dead, actors and directors do have a professional responsibility to consult with living playwrights about the production of their work whenever possible.

To sum up then, what is action? To act is to pursue inner action. What, then, is the relationship between inner action and external activity?

- Inner action may cause churning within but not exhibit conscious external behavior.
- Inner action emerges from a careful study of the given circumstances of the play.
- Inner action determines the character in the script but must never be confused with the personal concerns of the actor.
- The inner action that is part of a moment to moment flow of actions continues until the final curtain.
- Inner action delimits the kinds of external behavior and activities the actor will employ—the activities the audience will see and judge him by—including the way lines are said.
- Inner action is found in the drama of every culture.

Mastery of inner action releases every performer's gifts; ends anxiety; facilitates collaboration with fellow performers; makes the performance truthful, clearer, and more human; and leads to the possibility of hair-raising magical moments. I know of two superb texts on this subject that would be useful to any performer: Michael Shurtleff's *Auditioning,* which places a special emphasis on actions and exhorts actors to fight for the actions they choose, and *A Practical Handbook for the Actor* by Bruder et al., who give action the central place it deserves in the actor's work. In his introduction to *A Practical Handbook,* David Mamet writes,

> It is not up to you whether your performance will be brilliant—all that is under your control is your intention. It is not under your control whether your career will be brilliant—all that is under your control is your intention.[4]

A wise caution and practical advice. Of all the elements of the performance moment, the only one you can be sure to have totally under your control is your character's intention, the inner action.

Inner Action and the Interpretation of Text

2

I made the point late in the last chapter that the performer's interpretation of the playwright's work arises from an analysis of the given circumstances that leads to a choice of inner actions. That fact aside, there is a tendency in schools to teach interpretation of dramatic text using a literary model. And that's fine. But because theater studies and theater departments in the United States are mostly descended from English departments, many theater faculty members still approach drama as literary text. This perspective leads teachers to neglect concerns that are central to the performance of drama on stage. A script is not primarily a literary text. I prefer Jeffrey Sweet's description of a script in *The Dramatist's Toolkit* as a "program of opportunities for actors to do things designed to rivet the attention and sympathies of the audience."[5] It is precisely as a "program of opportunities for actors" that theater people—actors, directors, designers, critics, agents, and producers—have to concern themselves with the script and not treat that script as a literary text. Those who are concerned with the process of turning a script into performance have to see it as a structure of action.

Literary notions about the dramatic text are seldom concerned with a character's flow of inner actions; instead, literary analyses have traditionally focused on influences, themes, patterns of signs and images, relationships of themes to social context, and a host of other extratheatrical matters. These literary concerns have their value, but they are peripheral to the concerns of actors and directors preparing a script for production. Theater artists must concern themselves primarily with the structure of action based on the circumstances of the script. A traditional literary analysis can help after that task is completed.

The Structure of Action and Performance

Some will object that not all plays are like the classically structured dramas that I discuss here, which is true. However, we can often analyze stage pieces that are radically experimental from the point of view of inner action. Some might construe Robert Wilson's work as pageantry or spectacle. Heiner Müller's work might seem to defy categorization. A piece like The Living Theater's *Paradise Now* might seem wholly unamenable to the theories of Stanislavski. Nonetheless, all performers must search out precisely what it is their characters are struggling to do and must articulate the inner action—which may be nothing more than executing a list of activities because that is the director's instructions.

We could carry out an analysis of the structure of action in any piece—classical or experimental—in different ways. Stanislavski urged that we begin by finding the "through line" of action. If the playwright structured the piece around a character (a protagonist), I like to begin with a question such as, Whose play is it? and, What does that character want to do? That is to say, Who are the protagonists of the work? Although I acknowledge that Stanislavski's question about the through line of action is a more comprehensive question about the playwright's objective (which we have to know anyway), I am more confident about finding that objective after I've first found the protagonist.

I want to know which character's aspiration drives the dramatic action forward. I then need to know what obstacles or forces of antagonism the protagonist must confront. Rick in *Casablanca* wants desperately *to hide* from life but everything—enemies, friends, his lover—prevents him from doing so. He fails in his inner action and by failing becomes more of a human being. Petruchio in *The Taming of the Shrew* wants *to marry* a wealthy woman. Katherine confronts him with every impediment she can devise but he so charms and/or overwhelms her that she capitulates.

As a caution, move tentatively when identifying the protagonist. We can make a confident identification only after several close readings, preferably with actors. We should use the multiple readings to unlock and reveal the subtle circumstances that are hidden in, and sometimes only implied by, the text. We can easily mislead ourselves. Katherine, the "shrew," is a powerful character. It would be easy for some to decide that she is the protagonist of *The Taming of the Shrew* because she fights so hard to keep men at a distance. Others might decide that she wants *to maintain* her adolescent self-centered behavior. Some might say she is trying *to hide* her fear of growing up. However, if the director decides that Petruchio is the protagonist, which of these very different inner actions shall we choose for Katherine? The choice will define the character and the nature of the performance. A casual viewer of *Casablanca* could decide that Ilse, played by Ingrid Bergman, is the protagonist. She seems central to the piece and wants so much *to love* and *to win* Rick. It makes good sense to hold tentative the first identification of the protagonist. Continued work on the piece may yield new conclusions, especially when all the actors get involved exploring the possibilities of their assigned roles. Because the acting company as a whole has a major stake in the outcome of the project, involve everyone in the analysis of the script.

When we have tentatively identified a protagonist and decided what that character wants to do, we have taken an important first (if crude) step toward an interpretation of the play. Our decision about the protagonist's inner action will influence every subsequent decision about every other character and every moment in the play.

A literary analysis would take us in a very different direction. Questions that probe symbolic meanings might be asked: What does Petruchio signify in sixteenth-century England? What are the literary or historical sources for such a character? What does his behavior toward women tell us about gender interactions in the Renaissance? While these questions are fascinating and worthwhile, they are not fundamentally important to the actors. In fact, we know nothing of Petruchio's behavior until we make choices of inner action because they will solely determine the way the character will behave when the actor plays the part. If when they first meet in the play, the actor playing Petruchio decides he wants *to play* with Katherine, his behavior will be very different than if he decides that he wants *to dominate* her. Furthermore, his behavior would be different yet again if he decides he wants *to toy* with or *tease* her. The choice of the character's inner action determines the way the actor behaves as well as the meaning the actor gives to words.

Consider *Hamlet*. Suppose, after preliminary study, we decide that Hamlet is the protagonist—not much uncertainty about that—and that he wants *to avenge* his father's death. We feel confident of having found a valid inner action or superobjective. However, after working with actors and the script we might come to see that his inner action goes much deeper, that what he really wants to do is *purge* the state of its rottenness. This inner action demands something much more than mere vengeance. A performance governed by this inner action will be very different from one governed by the need *to avenge*. Because we made one decision about the single most important action in the script, both the lexical meaning of the words and their emotional burden will change. Stanislavski, by the way, is said to have chosen for Hamlet *to avenge* because seeking vengeance seemed a much more active, vivid, and vibrant inner action than *purging* the state.[6] I find that choice interesting because it suggests that Stanislavski, as a man of the theater, was more properly concerned with human dynamics on the stage than with exploring the deeper philosophical possibilities. Of course, I am not saying that the only possible superobjectives one might derive from Hamlet are *to avenge* or *to purge*. We might wish to explore other possibilities such as *to destroy*, *redeem*, *punish*, or *master* the situation. Each of these would certainly produce very different Hamlets. Exploring each of them in rehearsal would tend to deepen the actors' understanding of the play even if they were not chosen for performance.

Characters like Polonius, if developed under the influence of the vengeance interpretation, might be seen as mere obstacles to Hamlet's aspiration. On the other hand, if we see Hamlet as deciding *to purge* the body politic, the whole interpretation of the play changes. In the case of Polonius's murder, the actor playing Hamlet may, if he is concerned with revenge, slay the hidden Polonius because he believes the king is behind the arras. That action would color his activities during the murder in specific ways, perhaps tinging his behavior with glee. On the other hand, if Hamlet's primary inner action is *to cleanse* or *to purge* the state, the murder takes on an entirely different coloration. His motive or tactic for striking the person hidden there might become something like cleansing his mother's room, a room that we might see as a microcosm of the state. Hamlet's behavior in that case could well take on the stony detachment of an insect exterminator. Another actor might decide that Hamlet's task is *to defend* his mother from an unknown intruder or spy, an action resulting in yet another and different kind of behavior. In the case of the undone Ophelia, now a victim of the corrupt state, the actor might decide that Hamlet wants *to nurture* her. That would call for a very different behavior by an actor who in the vengeance mode might see her as a mere impediment. Change the inner actions and you change behavior, the meaning of the words, and the activities commanded by the script. It is actors who give life, force, and interpretation to words and to gesture.

After deciding on the protagonist's superobjective, we then determine the superobjectives of all the other characters guided by their relationship to the superobjective of the protagonist. What does Hamlet's uncle, the king, struggle to do? *Protect* himself from Hamlet? Look at his scenes from this perspective. What does Hamlet's mother want to do in the bedroom scene? *Dissuade* her son? What is the main objective of the character who is the driving force in each scene (who may not be the protagonist)? How does this objective relate to the other characters in these scenes?

We also need to find answers to these same questions for the parts that make up every scene. Just as bricklayers build walls with individual bricks, so do playwrights build scenes with individual sections called beats.[7] A new beat begins with a new action or a new mood, and we can identify new beats by that change of mood or action and often by the coming or going of a character.

The flow of action is not limited to one action per beat. A single speech might contain several actions. In *Angels in America,* for instance, Ron Leibman tells us that his director, George Wolfe, encouraged him to make his Roy Cohn less bludgeoning and more plaintive. That sounds as though Wolfe asked Leibman *to be* something—to be more plaintive. How does Leibman translate? "I'm playing the same notes," Leibman says, "But a lot of Roy's anger has become a kind of *pleading*." Note how he translates the director's suggestions into action, into verbs: "Instead of trying *to hit* Joe over the head, [Cohn is] trying *to make* him understand. Then when the boy *betrays* me, it hurts more."[8] By refining the flow of his inner actions, Leibman changes his lines from words that batter to words that cajole. It takes time and an open, exploratory attitude toward the text to establish the flow of changing inner actions from beginning to end. The work is hard, but it is the actor's preparatory business to choose, articulate, and establish the flow of actions for the entire play.

Leibman's control of the meaning of the text results from thinking about his lines in terms of the structure of action. His is not an intuitive approach and it's worth noting that his effort won him the Antoinette Perry Award in 1993 for his performance of Roy Cohn.

How the Actor Gives Meaning to Words

Think of the simple phrase "I love you." We have all played with phrases like it, placing emphasis on different words and deriving different meanings from them as in **I** love you, or I **LOVE** you, or I love **YOU**. But that is a mechanical and imprecise game. Consider how the words change meaning if what you really want to do is *to belittle* the person addressed. It might be something like "*I love you?*" If we really begin to think about giving meanings to those three little words, the possibilities are infinite. Try *to intimidate* with "I love you." Try *to convince, fool, condemn, love, insult,* and on and on. It is in this sense that the actor gives meaning to words and not the playwright. The responsibility for interpretation is usually thought to rest with the director but the director can only command a sure control of symbolic meanings inherent in the selection and the placement of actors and objects on the stage. The selection and use of colors and properties and certain matters of timing also fall under his responsibility. It is the actor who is in control of the meaning of words. This is why the actor is the central figure in theater. Every other member of a company just sets things up for actors to do. No matter how important we may imagine ourselves to be, the rest of us are just the actor's staff.

There is a scene in Bernard Pomerance's *Elephant Man* that nicely exemplifies what I have been saying about the structure of action. Treves, the physician, is my choice of the protagonist, not John Merrick, the actual "Elephant Man." The play is about Treves's aspiration *to outclass* the other medical scientists of his time. He chooses to help Merrick only because Merrick's illness makes him such an extraordinary specimen. Treves thinks that studying and writing about this "specimen" will help him to win the fame he so much wants.[9]

By scene 18, it is clear that Treves will fail to achieve his objective. Merrick proves himself too human to be a mere specimen. He is a sensitive, loving man, as well as intelligent, articulate, an artist, and perhaps a mystic. We will see this clearly in scene 18 when we find the doctor asleep and his patient at a lectern about to give a speech that mockingly parallels Treves's speech to the medical academy in scene 4, when Treves had said, "The most striking feature about him was his enormous head." Treves then proceeds to give a clinical description of Merrick's hideous malady in gruesome detail, never empathizing with his suffering humanity. Fourteen scenes later, Merrick gives a wonderfully ironic speech as Treves sleeps. I have shortened the actual monologue for convenience and inserted numbers to identify my choice of beats.

> MERRICK: (1) The most striking feature about him, note, is the terrifyingly normal head. This allowed him to lie down normally, and therefore to dream in the exclusive personal manner, without the weight of others' dreams accumulating to break his neck. From the brow projected a normal vision of benevolent enlightenment, what we believe to be a kind of self-mesmerizing state.
>
> (2) The mouth, deformed by satisfaction at being at the hub of the best of existent worlds, was rendered therefore utterly incapable of self-critical speech, thus of the ability to change. . . .
>
> (3) To add a further burden to his trouble, the wretched man when a boy developed a disabling spiritual duality, therefore was unable to feel what others feel, nor reach harmony with them.

How would I as an actor seeking Merrick's inner action analyze the structure of action in this monologue? Keep in mind that my thoughts are not a definitive analysis but an example of the process that I want to describe.

Having decided that Merrick is not the protagonist, I must decide what the function of his character is in the play. Is he a force of antagonism? A force working against Treves's wish for recognition? Yes, I think he provides obstacles to Treves's objective, but he is not an enemy. Merrick likes, maybe even loves, Treves. But Merrick—simply because he is a human being—stands in Treves's way. I see Merrick as a loving man and grateful to Treves. The question then becomes, What is Treves's action in this monologue?

First, I look to see if there are different subsidiary actions or tactics for each beat in that speech. There are. In beat 1 Merrick speaks of Treves's "terrifyingly normal head," his inability to dream of anything but himself, and his self-mesmerized conviction of benevolent enlightenment. I want Merrick *to mock*. I think my actor will find—knowing that he empathizes with Treves—a sadness in his mockery. Perhaps he may deliver his speech with a sad smile.

I think he might *scold* in the next beat, but I think it is a gentle scolding. There is anger in Merrick in this beat as well as sadness, but the self-satisfaction he accuses Treves of is not something Merrick finds in himself. In beat 2 I would choose *to scold* gently out of a love mixed with anger. I can hear somebody saying, "You said you don't worry about feelings and here you are talking about love mixed with anger." A good objection. Feelings are part of the given circumstances implied by the entire script. We have to decide, name, and choose what a character feels, but that is the intellect at work and is different from the pure, raw, emotional expression. The feelings I want Merrick to express will come automatically, arising out of inner action. I still need to name them but I can do that only after I know *to scold* is my inner action. Finally, for the third beat of Merrick's speech, I think I would choose *to comfort*. I would like to see sympathy in Merrick at this point. I want him *to comfort* the sleeping Treves.

To begin my exploration then, my choice of the main inner action in this speech might be *to commiserate* with the sleeping Treves and to get to that by *mocking*, *scolding*, and *comforting* him. I have thereby put the contents of the speech into the context of action. What does this do besides helping the actor find his own authentic and meaningful emotional expression? We have given a shape, a contour, a configuration to the monologue that helps the audience track with the actor and understand the interpretation.

Shaping speeches, beats, and scenes is an important part of the actor's work toward performance and must not be left entirely to directors. Shaping is an actor's contribution that arises directly from the use of the technique of inner action. Everybody knows the experience of sitting and listening to an actor work and sensing a feeling-full, believable performance while simultaneously forgetting almost instantly everything we've heard the actor say. It is as though the speech or the scene is composed of pearls fallen from a broken string. There is no shape to mere feeling-full performances. To engage and hold the audience's attention, there has to be a flow of connected actions, all of which arise from the given circumstances to clarify both cognitive and emotional meaning.

Consider another example, this time from Shakespeare. I suspect that were Gallup to take a poll he would find that most people consider Shakespeare's work the cultural equivalent of castor oil: It's good for you and you ought to take it. I can remember being a tenth grader in a Roman Catholic boys' school and having to go up to Father's desk and whisper in his ear so that other boys could not hear, "Tomorrow, and tomorrow, and tomorrow, creeps in this petty pace from day to day, To the last syllable of recorded time . . . of recorded time . . . uh."

"Did you memorize the speech, mister?"

"Uh, yes, Father, but . . ." WHAP across the right ear. "Mister, you have five minutes to go back to your desk and memorize this grand speech so that you will know it forever."

What did I learn from that? Not the speech; I still have to look it up. I learned to hate memorizing. I learned to avoid Shakespeare. I didn't learn from Father the skills I needed to find the extraordinary humanity in those plays.

How much more exciting it would have been had Father dealt with the entire twenty-three-line beat that begins with the moment Macbeth asks Seyton, "What is that noise?" Seyton answers, "It is the cry of women, my good Lord," and goes to investigate the problem, giving Macbeth the opportunity to muse alone about fear, something that haunts most boyish dreams, when he says, "The time has been my senses would have cool'd to hear a night-shriek, and my fell of hair would at a dismal treatise rouse and stir as life were in't." Night fright! The very stuff of adolescence. A shriek at night would make the hair on the back of his head rise. Every kid can relate to that.

Then Macbeth goes on to say, "I have supp'd full with horrors; Direness, familiar to my slaughterous thoughts, cannot once start me." Wouldn't it have been interesting to figure out what this might mean? "I have supp'd full with horrors." Imagine helping kids to see the image of a man eating the horrible and murderous things he has done. Then, "Direness, [Get the dictionary. It means 'horror.'] familiar to my slaughterous thoughts [Bring *that* imagery to life.], cannot once start me." What does that mean? Look up *start.* My dictionary refers to "a sudden, brief shock or fright; a startled reaction." He is saying that he's lived with so much horrible slaughter that it doesn't bother him anymore and it can't even startle him! What does he *mean* by that? Is he sadly *confessing* to himself that he is numb? Is he *denying* what he really feels to protect himself from another feeling? Is he *bragging*? Kids could have great fun with questions like these, taking the given circumstances they have found in the play and finding inner actions that are meaningful. And we haven't even gotten to "Tomorrow, and tomorrow . . ."

Let's stay with this for a moment more. Seyton returns and Macbeth asks, "Wherefore was that cry?" *Wherefore?* How many get that word wrong? There are many people who think that when Juliet cries out, "O Romeo, Romeo! Wherefore art thou, Romeo?" she is peering out into the garden searching for him, wondering where he is. She is musing, asking sadly, "Why are you named Romeo?" *Wherefore* means *why*. It doesn't have anything to do with location. We have to make sure we know the lexical meaning of Shakespeare's words.

So Macbeth is asking Seyton *why*. Why was there a cry? He is told flatly that, "The Queen, my lord, is dead." No mincing around with Seyton: "The screaming means your wife's dead." And what does Macbeth say? Does he get upset? Not likely. Instead, he says what may be the most extraordinary thing in this whole beat, a statement that Father didn't even think worth our attention: "She should have died hereafter; there would have been time for such a word." Whoa! That seems cold, even chilling. What does it mean? Back in the dictionary, we find that *hereafter* means "the future." It also carries a second meaning of "after death," which suggests a pun: she should have died after death? What does that mean? The kids would by now be doing mental calisthenics! Let's get them back to focusing on the inner action.

What is Macbeth doing when he says that she should have died in the future, that there would have been time for such a word? We'll find out what he means when we find out what he is doing. Is he *brooding*? Is he *mocking*? What is his feeling state? Is he depressed? Is this some kind of graveyard humor? Is he truly numb? Or is this an expression of grief? Is he *grieving*? Or is he, in the depth of his misery, *shaping* Seyton's vision of the value of life: "She should have died at another time, there is plenty of time to die. Life is meaningless, a shadow, a strutting and fretting player soon gone from the stage." I think we could have played all of those Macbeths in school that day. By doing so we would have felt the excitement and vitality embodied in that short beat, a vitality that would have given us a clue to the magical, quintessentially human mind of William Shakespeare. Instead, Father bopped our ears because we failed to memorize something we didn't understand. Father was irresponsible. He should have guided us into the work, shown us how to use the dictionary. He should have shown us how to piece together the evidence of the play, how to find the inner actions, and how to listen ("And what of the name *Seyton?* Do you boys think that Shakespeare never noticed that it rhymes with *Satan?*"). Instead he made us all wonder wherefore in hell we were reading this peculiar stuff anyway.

An extraordinary thing happens when people find themselves solving the problems of Shakespearean language and style: the work becomes marvelously accessible, familiar, human, real, truthful, and entertaining. But a joyful introduction to Shakespeare's work rarely happens. If the conventional attitudes of the general population toward Shakespeare are any guide, the revelation of his magic seldom happens in performance and, in my opinion, happens even less often in school. Why? One reason is that naive hearers of the work have had the misfortune of listening to teachers who didn't care about the work! Another reason is that they've listened to actors who are more in love with the sound of their own voices than with the actions that define Shakespeare's characters.

I offer an hypothesis for making Shakespeare accessible to reasonably intelligent adolescents and adults. The following process will produce a performance that audiences will fully understand even when they do not know the explicit meaning of the words. First, know the dictionary meaning of every word you say in the text. Second, conduct a careful analysis of the given circumstances and develop an understanding of the emotional freight carried by every word. Finally, apply this carefully developed comprehension of the text to the technique of inner action. No actor will mislead her audience if she knows what *wherefore* means both cognitively and emotionally.

If we follow this process carefully and if we choose vivid inner actions and if we act the part spontaneously, Shakespeare's text will engage, entertain, and hold the most untutored audience. The actor may cut text but must not change a word. We will require no programs or footnotes. Our actors will do what our actors do best. The actress playing Juliet who knows that she is to complain wistfully about the lovely boy's name will signal the meaning of *wherefore* and the audience will just know that she means "Why?"

Kenneth Branagh's productions of *Much Ado About Nothing* and *Henry V* offer vivid examples of the results of this procedure. One may not agree with all of Branagh's choices or all of his casting, but one will note that the audience hears the text. In these films the audience understands the text and remains engaged by the performances. The test of Branagh's understanding of inner action is evident in his performance of *Henry V*. Olivier's performance of Henry betrays his concern with other matters. This concern results in a performance that is flamboyant and colorful but filled with dialogue that causes me to drift and daydream. The old literary notion of the intentional fallacy aside, I think Olivier wanted *to impress* us rather than to reveal the inner actions of the characters. Branagh's directorial objective was to find and work with those inner actions.

To my mind the usages in *Lear* are among the most difficult to master in all of Shakespeare. The following passage is one of those speeches that tempts actors to oratorical grandiloquence and pomposity and sends an audience into daydreams. In act 2, scene 4, Goneril and Regan have cut down the king's bodyguard by half and then down to twenty-five when Regan finally asks him, "What need one?" (Again I've numbered the beats as I choose to recognize them.) Lear replies,

> (1) O, reason not the need! (2) Our basest beggars
> Are in the poorest thing superfluous.
> (3) Allow not nature more than nature needs,
> Man's life is cheap as beast's. (4) Thou art a lady:
> (5) If only to go warm were gorgeous,
> Why, nature needs not what thou gorgeous wear'st,
> Which scarcely keeps thee warm. (6) But, for true need—
> (7) You heavens, give me that patience, patience I need!

These are only nine of twenty-three lines in this monologue, but they are enough to illustrate my point. To begin with, we can readily see that the speech presents problems. Read it through as though it were prose and it makes almost no sense. By the ninth line most readers will not know what they have read. In conventional Shakespearean acting, one might initially think it sheer bombast: "O, reason not the need!" We can almost hear those familiar resonances, those fine Oxbridgian tones—those actors imitating actors imitating actors back to Irving and beyond. In other words, we are all too familiar with the posturing and pretentious would-be acting that lines like these encourage. Anything that turns off an audience is not acting and can never be more than "would be acting." Consider instead the circumstances of the script.

Lear has been the most privileged of men. Preeminent among those privileges has been his right to a hundred-man bodyguard—feudal vassals who love him and would give up their lives for his. They were a hundred friends who went everywhere with him, played with him, served him body and soul, and laughed at his dullest jokes. They were men to whom he in turn was gladly obligated. But now his daughters say he can't have them with him anymore. Budgets? Suddenly he is powerless and alone. Best friends? Life's companions? Mere "girls" can't do that! But these children are powerful women. One must act in a politic way with them despite their insensitivity. What to do? Well, apparently he cannot simply rant, scold, and harangue these two women. And let's be smart about this: actorish posturing will not convince these women. To posture them into changing their minds is silly, and yet we've watched generations of actors do just that. I think this cunning old wolf wants *to disarm* these female children by charming them, wooing them into submission.

I have divided this part of the monologue into seven beats. That means that I intend to use seven different tactics to achieve the main objective of disarming the daughters. As an actor I really want to charm and disarm my two colleagues on stage. I want them to feel my charm. I want to see them become warm and affectionate. That will really feed their determination to exact their price from this old blackguard who probably never gave them a warm, fatherly hug in his long life; for why else would they treat him so shabbily?

Here is one set of possible choices of action for these seven beats.

Beat 1: "O, reason not the need!" I want to appeal to the daughters' generosity in a sweet and loving and fatherly way as in, "Sweetheart, it's not need." Take her hand. *Appeal.*
Beat 2: "Our basest beggars Are in the poorest thing superfluous." In other words, even the poorest of us have more than we need. *Agree* with her nonverbally. *Disarm* her by agreeing with her, sadly.
Beat 3: "Allow not nature more than nature needs, Man's life is cheap as beast's." *Validate* her thinking and choices with your experience and wisdom.
Beat 4: "Thou art a Lady." *Honor* her person, her intelligence, her wisdom.
Beat 5: "If only to go warm were gorgeous, Why nature needs not what thou gorgeous wear'st, Which scarcely keeps thee warm." This is one of those passages that makes readers fade in confusion. I think the burden is simply, "You don't wear gorgeous, low-necked silk (rather than thick wool) dresses to keep yourself warm: You wear them to look beautiful." He is frankly validating their beauty, *flattering* them. Fatherly flattery ought to get father somewhere with his daughters. It ought make them see that even their beauty is no preparation

for combat with the cold world, just as his royalty is nothing without his comrades.

Beat 6: "But, for true need—" He begins to make an intellectual distinction between real necessity and kingly accoutrements, but he sees it isn't working. He can't charm them. He stops himself and *shifts*. And the action of shifting takes place in the silence between beats 6 and 7! We do not limit the flow of action to words.

Beat 7: "You heavens, give me that patience, patience I need!" Does he pray? Not *my* Lear. He wrestles with himself, *takes control* of himself and says, "Careful. Take another tack with these two. This approach isn't working."

Summing up then, *to disarm* Regan and Goneril, Lear tries several tactics: he *appeals*, *agrees*, *validates*, *flatters*, and *honors* them only to realize it isn't working, which causes him *to shift* his approach and *wrestle* himself under control. Executed by a sensitive actor who is truly living those actions, Shakespeare's words will make sense to the audience. The actor will engage the audience with his work. I repeat: the actor who knows the sequential flow of action, the meaning of the words, and the feeling states of his character will enact a Shakespearean role in a way that will make the meaning clear and dynamic for even a naive audience.

I have only illustrated the process with these two abbreviated monologues. The actor's task is to apply the process to the entire play. It is what Stanislavski meant when he talked about "scoring" a script: searching out the structure of action and articulating the flow of inner action based on given circumstances. We could do more. We could, for instance, consider the various physical activities that could accompany each action. We might do that at our desk or in workshop with other actors. Consider scoring a guide, part of the discovery process, a flexible guide that may change. It is a guide that the actor plays with and learns thoroughly in rehearsal so that he will not have to think about it in performance.

Inner Action in The Seagull

One way to look at the bare bones plot of Chekhov's richly textured play is to follow the loves of two women: Masha, daughter of Madame Arkadina's farm manager, and Nina, a young and naive neighbor who wants to go to the city and become a successful actress. Masha is deeply in love with Trepleff, Mme. Arkadina's son and a would-be writer, but he barely notices Masha. Trepleff is intent on Nina, who is infatuated with Trigorin, Mme. Arkadina's lover. Trigorin is a successful writer and womanizer who seduces Nina away to Moscow for what proves to be a short-lived romance that ends up very badly for Nina. In the course of events Masha, while always yearning for Trepleff, marries Medvedenko, bears his child, and lives with him with growing contempt. Young Trepleff, having lost Nina to Trigorin, immerses himself hermitlike in his writing where he finds some success but continues to yearn for Nina. After a certain interval we learn that all their lives have come to unhappiness. At last, after a short and unexpected encounter with the unhappy Nina, who is searching for Trigorin, Trepleff shoots himself. We learn about this event when we are told in the last speech that the knowledge of his suicide should be kept from his mother.

Who is the protagonist? Who struggles desperately from beginning to end to accomplish something? Who faces the most obstacles? I find that Trepleff, not the two young women who also face obstacles to their objectives, is the central focus of the play. He wants Nina. Masha wants him. His Uncle Sorin supports him on his estate while he seeks success as a writer. His mother, Mme. Arkadina, treats him with indifference. Meanwhile, Trigorin cheats on Arkadina by having an affair with Nina, his chosen love, who tolerates him with indifference. He stands like the hub toward which the other principals generate their actions. What is his principal action, his superobjective?

There are several possibilities we might consider. He wants *to win* Nina. He wants *to succeed* as a writer. He wants *to win* approval. Why does he pursue each of these actions? All of these are accurate Trepleff actions, but is any one of them his superobjective? No, his superobjective enfolds all these. And what might that be? *To win* respect. When we begin the preparation of this performance by focusing on Trepleff's struggles *to win* the world's respect for his writing, the love and respect of his mother, the respect of his stepfather and of his neighbors, the love and respect of Nina, and most of all the struggle for self-respect, we find ourselves on the right track toward the final resolution when we learn that he, in his own opinion, has failed. He then kills himself.

This is gloomy stuff. These people lead gloomy lives. Masha always wears black. Medvedenko can't earn enough money to feed his household. Mme. Arkadina is weary living a life of ennui and will debase herself to keep Trigorin who, while famous, unhappily dislikes his own obsessiveness and his work. Nina loses her love and her baby and the possibility of stardom. The farm manager bullies Arkadina. Her brother Sorin, the owner of the estate, is old and worn out and bored with life at sixty. It isn't a crowd that would make for a very lively night at the theater, yet it is one of the greatest of modern classics. Why? What do we have to do to make it work?

The success of the piece depends on *how* we play the actions of these apparently morose characters. It is at this juncture that the director comes into the business of dealing with the technique of inner action.

Acting: Beyond the Text

The task isn't finished when the actor chooses his inner action. He also has his director to deal with. Do they agree? If so, *how* will the actor play that action? Like any verb, the inner action is susceptible to the influence of adverbs. For every action we choose, we must decide how we will play that action and the director should take part in that decision.

If the director's choice is that the actors should play all that gloominess in *The Seagull* in a gloomy way, she will have made a bad choice. For one thing, it will make all the characters look like they are indulging in their sorrows. Audiences do not like to watch self-pity. We want to see characters struggling against their heartache. Furthermore, self-pity is low energy while struggle expresses high energy. The characters in this play have to play against their woe. They have to deny it. Even as they say the saddest of their lines, they must say them with a smile or even laughter. Chekhov's characters laugh at their anguish.

The choices André Gregory, Louis Malle, and their cast made for *Vanya on Forty-Second Street* provide excellent examples of smiling denial. The actors in this film *deny* with smiles and laughter the anguish they are living. The result is a wonderfully accessible version of *Uncle Vanya*.

Consider the opening beat of *The Seagull*. It is a mere matter of about ten speeches between Masha and Medvedenko. He begins the play by asking Masha, the woman he wants to win, why she always wears black. She tells him she is in "mourning for her life. I'm unhappy." When he replies that his "life is much harder than hers," we should remember that his action is *to woo* even though he feels overburdened with responsibilities. She changes the subject and reminds him that a play will soon begin. He tells her that Nina and Trepleff will present it. We don't know it yet, but the not-very-smart Medvedenko—who has come to woo Masha—is reminding his would-be love that in just a moment she will see her true love working with her rival! In the meantime, Medvedenko complains about how much he loves Masha, how she won't oblige him, how far he has to walk to see her, how little he has, and who wants to marry a man with nothing. She dismisses his efforts, telling him that his love touches her but that she can't return it and offers him snuff.

What are the inner actions? In my mind, her's is *to tolerate* the poor man until the play written by Trepleff, the man she dearly loves, begins. Medvedenko's is *to capture* her love by winning her sympathy. The problem presented to the actors and the director by this beat is simply this: If you play these actions as though the words they say are all the characters mean, you will alienate the audience. The audience does not want to relate to characters that seem to indulge their own morose inclinations. They want to see them struggle against their sadness. The subtext is what is important and the subtext that I choose is *to play*. Masha might want *to tolerate* the man and he might want *to capture* her, but they are not going to reveal these true aspirations. They are going *to play* with each other. They can say the saddest things to each other and engage us because we see them denying their heartache. Actors playing this scene must not enact this beat in solemn seriousness. Malle, Gregory, Wallace Shawn, and the rest of the *Vanya* cast make this choice brilliantly.

Consider the first two lines of *The Seagull*[10]:

MEDVEDENKO: Why do you always wear black?
MASHA: I am in mourning for my life. I'm unhappy.

Productions of this play choosing to open with the saddest and most morose expressions possible make a bad choice. It is a choice that makes it hard for us to empathize with such self-pitying people. Let's imagine that the actors are working against the literal meaning of the words they are saying, even seeming to deny what they are saying. Imagine that the actor playing Medvedenko decides *to tease* her and says with a searching and friendly smile, "Why do you always wear black?" His emphasis might fall on *you*, perhaps hinting that it is so unlikely that she would make such a choice. It might fall on *always*, suggesting his incredulity that a woman as lovely as she would *always* make such a choice. An actor wanting *to tease* or *to play* could find surprising and spontaneous ways of doing so using his own choice of word emphasis or inflection. The effect would be to feed the actress with a wonderful potential for spontaneous teasing in her turn.

I can imagine her laughing aloud, perhaps pinching him playfully on the arm as she says, "I am mourning for my life." Then she laughs even more merrily, saying, "I'm unhappy." What happens in the audience? They believe her *and* they admire her for her feistiness. They would also see that she is not attached to this man who is trying to relate to her so clumsily. The actors might just win the audience's empathy with these tactics. That is a large load for two lines. It is also another example of how actors give meaning to words.

It is at this point, well after decisions about inner actions have been taken and will be executed, that the director begins to block the show. The most artful blocking connects with the entire flow of inner actions, clarifying and enhancing them. In the first two lines of *The Seagull* we learn that the characters are returning from a walk.

But how? Our knowledge of their inner actions tells us, and we have decided that they are returning playfully. Does that mean they walk side by side? Only if that enhances the chosen inner actions. Perhaps we'll have them come on separately with Medvedenko running onto the stage to turn around to gaze at her hopefully as she comes into view. As she approaches, he holds out his arms to embrace her while saying, "Why do you always wear black?" But, laughing—at his clumsy attempt to embrace her or at herself?—she deftly avoids his arms and sweeping past him merrily lets him know that she is "in mourning for my life." As she whirls past him, she dismisses him and herself with a happy wave of her hand saying, "I'm unhappy."

Inner Action and the Theater Community

If Petruchio struggles *to woo* Katherine, he will not move in relation to her in the same way he might if he tries *to intimidate* her. Even if he says that he wants *to intimidate* her but we know from the subtext that he really wants *to woo*, appropriate blocking will illuminate the true inner action. The director reveals the true relationships of the characters to the audience using their inner actions as a guide. Directors should embrace the technique of inner action. The more the director works with the structure of action and plays with possible choices of action the more she will find in the script to illuminate the script. If she works with her actors to analyze and articulate inner actions, she will evoke richer and more authentic performances from those actors.

André Gregory's directorial choices in *Vanya* validate my point about *The Seagull*. We all know what it is *to deny* sadness with smiles, and *Vanya* moves us closer to those nineteenth-century Russians so that we empathize with them. The choice *to deny* is effective because Gregory and Malle have revealed what the playwright has deliberately hidden. Playwrights hide inner realities. Their characters, like real people, frequently say "I will" when they mean "I won't." The best directorial choices reveal the true hidden meaning—the subtext—of each moment.

There is an element in the structure of action that I have not mentioned that is particularly relevant to the work of directors though actors must not ignore it, either. Some call it the *cap* of a scene, while the ancients called it the *catastrophe.* I call it the *event.* There is an "event" in every scene. If there is no event there is no scene and no drama—just a passage of dialogue, a slice of life, and a bit of talk.

I identify the event as that precise moment in a scene that tells us the meaning of the scene. These scene events lead in turn to the principal event of the play—the catastrophe. When Hamlet kills the king, we see the principal event of the play. We learn that he has avenged his father's murder and/or purged the state, depending on your interpretation. There is an event in every scene leading up to that moment. In act 3, scene 3 of *Hamlet,* Rosencrantz and Guildenstern meet with the king. He tells them that he doesn't like Hamlet and feels unsafe with the madman. He is, therefore, sending the two of them to accompany Hamlet to England. He repeats that his throne is insecure because of Hamlet's lunacy. Guildenstern replies, "We will ourselves provide," signaling with those four words that he has agreed to assassinate Hamlet. *That is the event of the scene.* Not a word about murdering Hamlet has been spoken. It is all indirection. The words continue to flow after Guildenstern's line, rushing in a great rococo gush of rhetoric. If the actors and director want the audience to know these characters and the purpose of this scene, the director and actors must mark the event and highlight it in some way. How? A pause. A look. A smile. A handshake. Whatever works, whatever tells us that Rosencrantz and Guildenstern have agreed to the king's wish that they kill the prince while accompanying him to England. They have one moment to do it. That moment is the event.

Sometimes the event of a scene is difficult to find. Sometimes just identifying the event defines the meaning of the entire play. What is the event in *The Taming of the Shrew?* Is it Katherine's speech at the end when she yields to her husband and urges all other women to do the same? If so, the play must be a paean to male dominance. And it certainly isn't that. Does it happen when she brings on the errant wives at Petruchio's command? No— Katherine and Petruchio are comrades by then. We know she will do that. What *is* the event in the play?

If Petruchio is the protagonist and he wants to win Katherine, the event in the play comes at the very moment when we learn for sure whether he has won her, which takes place in act 4 when they are on the road to Padua. Petruchio notices the sun and says how brightly shines the moon, and Katherine contradicts him telling him he is looking at the sun. They argue and having had enough, he orders their party to return to his house. Hortensio begs her to "say as he says," at which point Katherine yields totally: "Forward, I pray since we have come so far." Is that the event? No, since she could still be in opposition. But then she says, "And be it moon, or sun, or what you please. And if you please to call it a rush candle, Henceforth I vow it shall be so for me." The moment Katherine makes that vow is the event in *The Taming of the Shrew.* The rest of act 4 and all of 5 merely work out the power won by this pair of lovers compared to the other characters in the play. Or better, we might regard the rest of the play as fulfilling what I prefer to interpret as the playwright's primary objective, which is to show the power of mature love. I don't want to believe that Shakespeare urged the abuse of women.

Over the last thirty or forty years auteur theory has become fashionable among directors, tempting many to ignore the playwright and do any damn thing with the script they please. There is an idea out there that playwrights are theatrically inept and possessed of flawed vision. Directors have to see that the key to their work with the script is in the inner action. We should not decide where to move actors simply because of vague notions of stage imagery or timing or "how good" the move feels. Ignoring inner action leads to arbitrary and irrelevant choices. It is bad directorial craft.

No Scene Without an Event,
No Event Without an Inner Action

Sometimes the playwright is entirely dependent on the director to reveal the meaning of the scene. The subtext—the conflict—is so hidden as to make the surface of the interactions seem entirely bland and undramatic. Imagine that two neighbors happen to meet in front of the post office. They shake hands, and Charles greets Mike.

> CHARLES: Mike! Haven't seen you around. Where've you been?
> MIKE: Oh, hiya, Charley! Oh, a lotta gardening. You know, problems with water. No rain.
> CHARLES: Still carrying water? Saw Ann today.
> MIKE: Oh, yeah? The water company can bring it in and I can pay for it but you know the problem.
> CHARLES: No. What's that?
> MIKE: They'd have to run the line across the northeast corner of your place, Charles. And I just don't . . .
> CHARLES: Oh, come on, neighbor! You've gotta have water.
> MIKE: Yeah. Well, if you see Ann, tell her I said hello.
> CHARLES: You take care now, Mike.

You might read this and wonder what it's all about. It's just small talk; even the water problem doesn't seem urgent. They talk about the weather, about gardening, about someone passing by. They say good-bye. A typical small-town or neighborly encounter at the post office. If the director reads it and decides there is no inner action but chatting, that nothing happens, he has to decide that it is a badly written scene—that it is no scene at all. If he trusts the playwright he will look carefully at the clues and see if there is conflict. He will try to find out just what it is that the two characters want to accomplish.

There are little clues in the interaction that tell me that Mike wants to win his neighbor's permission and that Charles takes an ambiguous position. And who is Ann? There is a tension around Ann. They say innocuous words, but those words seem freighted beyond their overt meaning, especially that last line when, after Mike asks Charles to remember him to Ann, Charles evasively answers with "You take care now." I see competition between these two. They are both interested in Ann for some reason and Mike needs permission from Charles to run a water line through his property. Is Charles's action *to warn* Mike about his relationship with Ann when he says, "You take care now"? If so, the action of warning impregnates the scene with meaning and "You take care now" becomes an event. From the beginning of the scene Mike's action is *to win* Charles's permission for a water line. Charles's action is *to warn* Mike about Ann.

If we now put all of this into performance the audience will sense conflict immediately from the behavior of the actors that arises from those inner actions. More than that, the audience will want to watch, wondering what will happen until they hear Charles's warning, the event. The audience is now set up for their next encounter, and they will want to see how these two deal with their strained relationship.

If the inner actions had not been played or if both actors had merely stopped to chat, there would have been no drama and no event. As we've seen before, playing inner action clarifies subtext that would otherwise be lost, with the consequence that the scene could well have no consistent meaning. Inner action makes this conflict apparent by determining the way the character takes his leave and enacts the event.

It is the actor's responsibility in working with the director to identify both the central action of a scene and the event and to do whatever is necessary to make both clear to the audience. If we do not highlight the event, the audience will not know what the scene is about and its meaning will be lost. The *way* Charles breaks off and says his final line is what gives the scene its meaning. If we do not clarify the event, if the moment is not understood as an event, the audience will interpret the passage as nothing but idle chitchat. The marking I'm calling for may very well not be in the script. Shakespeare doesn't tell us to emphasize that moment when Guildenstern agrees to assassinate Hamlet. The director and the actor have to see it, realize its importance, and make us know that this is what the scene is all about. We can highlight the event with nothing more than a gesture invented by the actor, a wink, a toss of a hand, a shrug, or even a moment of silence. The possibilities are endless.

The Simplest Things Are the Hardest to Master

One of the easiest things for most people to do is say what we want to do. Or is it? Persons coming to the craft of inner action for the first time often find the technique difficult to master. They are often people who had wonderful success the first time they performed on stage. They discover they have talent. Suddenly, filled with enthusiasm, they want to go on and do more and maybe—such fools we mortals are—become full-time professional actors. They sign up for an acting class where they meet someone who tells them to learn to work with objectives: "Figure out what your character wants to do, find the action, articulate it, and do it."

Simple. Except for some it isn't so easy and they resist, wanting only to work intuitively. As I pointed out earlier, they often seem to know their character's objective on some level but don't know how to put that knowledge into words. Part of us knows what we want to do, but until we articulate it we are not in full control, not focused, and not quite sure. We lack a solid grasp of the objective. We need words, and until we put the flow of inner action into words we are at the mercy of wild talent. Like all craft, the purpose of the technique of inner action is to put a bridle on that wildness so that it will behave as and when we wish. More than that, acting is a process that requires the deepest searching into our own creative resources. It is not an idle hobby, a game of small worth, or an entertainment for our ego. To act is to take on a responsibility to audiences and self, to fellow actors, to the director and playwright, and to all the members of the theater company. The responsible actor demands the mastery of craft.

Sometimes newcomers who have some success working intuitively find mastering inner action frustrating. They often persuade themselves that it is unnecessary to master a technique that requires them to articulate those easy, intuitive choices. After all, these novices may have worked with directors who, not being proficient with the technique of the inner action, never said a word about it. Why should they bother if directors don't care? In their experience, analysis may have been limited to how a character feels or what a character wants to be. While we want to know these important circumstances, knowing them is only part of the task. The actor also has to articulate the flow of inner action. She may have heard talk about knowing the character's background. She may do research. But she must learn that to consider circumstances without articulating actions will lead her to experience performance as imprecise and mystifying. Precision, control, surprising and creative possibilities, and consistency come only with the exploration of inner actions.

As we noted earlier, lacking a clear articulation of what the character's inner action is, the naive actor will probably go onto the stage encumbered with objectives like trying to feel, trying to remember blocking and lines, trying to do everything right, and trying to impress. The mystery is that sometimes—these distracting objectives aside—wild talent performs marvelously. Sometimes.

Newcomers to performance often seem to think that acting teachers in scene class know and teach the "correct" interpretation of a scene. Sad to say, there are teachers who believe in "correct" interpretations. They lead actors to believe that they can succeed by imitating someone else or by slavishly following a teacher's interpretation of a play. Too often the result of that kind of teaching in scene class is to condition the actor to impress or to get it "right." These become unconscious objectives that retard student progress. Effective teachers discourage these purposes and help students to learn a technique to develop their own authority.

When students take their first steps with this process and are asked to identify only the superobjective of a character, they learn easily and exhibit little resistance. However, when we ask the beginner to articulate the character's inner action for each scene and for each beat within each scene and to find the appropriate events as well, resistance grows. The urge to rebel surfaces. Students of all ages begin to grumble and say, "Hey, what's the use of this? I can do it better when I never think of this stuff!" The acting teacher may then waver and say, "Well, maybe there is an easier way, maybe they can get this later. Maybe they can do it better without this stuff about objectives and inner actions. I give up. Let's do some sensory exercises."

This is an ineffective approach. People are simply not accustomed to clarifying and articulating their own objectives in terms of action. Ask many young people what they want "to do" and too often the reply is a noun like actor, lawyer, or teacher. We're often conditioned to think of *being* something instead of *doing* something. If an acting teacher has any responsibility at all, it is to make the naive actor understand the need to think in terms of action. We must make the mastery of this fundamental technique a priority.

"What do you want to be when you grow up?" "I don't know—be a neurosurgeon or maybe a police officer." "Well, if you could *do* whatever you wanted, what would you do?" "Be rich!" Think about it. When asked what we want to do, we respond with what we want to be. The question, What do you want to do? goes unheard or overwhelms. When beginning students are pressed to answer with an action the most frequent response I see is a blank face and a frustrated "I don't know!" accompanied, perhaps, by an unspoken resentment for having been pressed.

With new actors the consequence of this cultural tendency is that they turn their thoughts to what a character is or wants to be. They think of the work from the audience's perspective: "She wants to be his lover." "He is hunchbacked and cruel." Actors need to practice thinking from an actor's point of view: What is the action? To what does she aspire? *To win* him. What does he want to do? To rescue the maiden. As I pointed out earlier, one consequence of actors thinking from the audience's perspective is stereotyping. If an actor goes on stage to be a hunchbacked and cruel king, *to be* becomes Richard III's objective, and that is just plain wrong because his action is *to amass* power. Actors have to know what their actions are. To do otherwise is to see talented people going on stage to perform stereotypes based on clichés about cruel hunchbacks. These clichés pale in comparison with the exciting possibilities the actor can reveal if he explores *Richard III* with the techniques of inner action.

In my experience, actors unfamiliar with this technique most often balk because it is the process of articulating—finding the right words for their inner actions—that is most difficult. They seem to know on some level what the character wants to achieve or fight for: "I know what I want to do. I just can't say it. I can't find the words for it." "Does he want to kiss her?" "No, that is not it." "Does he want to protect her?" "No. He doesn't really like her." "So, what does he want to do?" "I don't know!" "You seem to know what he doesn't want!" "Yes." "So, what does he want?" "Well . . . well . . . maybe he wants to get power over her?" "OK, maybe. Anything else?" "Yeah! He wants *to use* her to get more power!" "See, you knew." "Yeah, but boy, this is hard."

Like any skill, we will find the task easier when we persevere. The knowledge may be in us, lodged and inarticulate in our brain. We may find in our first attempts on stage that we have an easy but uncertain facility. When some actors first begin to use the technique of inner action, they stumble and feel that it has let them down. Discouraged, they want to stop. However, if encouraged to persist, if given the opportunities to see that actions encourage their creativity and magic, students will soon find the motivation to work through the hard part. "First there is a mountain, then there is no mountain, then there is"—an old Donovan song, an older Zen proverb.

When supported and challenged, students come to recognize that this basic skill gives them a more satisfactory control and opens them to a more passionate and exciting performance. They accept that they have to go through a period when they'll feel lost and clumsy. They will also find an additional, unsought benefit as they begin to use the technique in other aspects of their lives. They will discover that the best way to set goals is not to think of being something ("I want to be a firefighter") but to articulate actions ("I want to fight fires," "I want to serve my community," or "I want to develop myself as a competent, professional performer").

The Technique of Inner Action is a Creative Process

The best way to effect the transition from awkwardness to facility is to encourage actors to play with the text in the most outrageous, unlikely, unsettling ways possible. Play with that text in ways that would send English teachers and other curators of culture into panic. Turn it upside down and backwards, but always play with articulated character actions no matter how wrong or unlikely they might seem. Never tolerate mere states of being. Furthermore, go with whatever behavioral impulses rise to the surface—go with your impulses—so long as they don't interfere with or hurt your partners in the scene. By playing with the possibilities in the text actors learn both to master the technique and inevitably to study and discover the many possibilities within the script.

In other words, having accepted the idea of working with inner actions and learning to deal with the structure of action and the circumstances of the text, after working with all those newly found actions, violate the best choices. Articulate inner actions that look to be the very opposite of what the characters seem to be doing. Explore objectives that seem downright wrong.

What would happen if, while exploring the script's possibilities, the actor decided to play with the notion that Hamlet stabs Polonius because he wants *to love* the old man? Outrageous? Wrong? Sure. What would happen if—in stabbing Polonius—his inner action is *to intimidate* his mother (not all that unlikely)? Surprising creative possibilities would present themselves. While the *performance* choice may be neither *to love* nor *to coerce*, playing with unlikely choices in rehearsal provides new insights, new discoveries that take actors (and anyone interested in the play) deeper into the text. Playing with actions takes us closer to our own truth and further from stereotyping or mere imitation. The technique of the inner action is a creative process.

For the performer to play with this process is to experience a rising tide of creative excitement that reinforces a willingness to master the technique. By playing with the process, we learn to conquer the seeming obscurity of the script with a tool of incomparable penetrating power. Everybody benefits. Student actors find a method to uncover fresh meaning and feeling in words. Skilled actors and directors using the playful approach in rehearsals discover new possibilities and enrich the rehearsal process. In fact, this is the way to prevent deadening repetition in rehearsal. Everybody who plays with inner actions will find themselves sharpening their ability to articulate actions while deepening their overall comprehension of the work.

Mastering the Entire Flow of Actions Within a Scene

The next level of difficulty arises when the actor begins to score the entire flow of inner actions within a scene. Many students resist this step because it requires thinking, guessing, stumbling, uncertainty, and very close work with the text. It means that we decide to set ourselves to the task of learning to articulate knowledge held subverbally in our brain.

One problem often arises from previous training. For example, many people have been taught that the building blocks of scenes, those short sections of dialogue we call beats, are the same as French scenes. Others learn that beats are the moments between character entrances and exits. Other teachers say that beats are those small sections between mood changes. I prefer to speak in terms of the structure of action and describe beats as the building blocks of scenes in which the tactics or subactions of scenes shift and change. Richard III may want to use Anne, but he won't show her that. While Richard's main objective or inner action may be *to conquer* her, he begins softly as though *to flatter*: "Sweet saint, for charity, be not so curst." But as she resists he will change his tactics and gradually work on her with several actions including *persuading*, *charming*, and even *threatening*. And more. All in one scene. That flow of constantly changing inner action goes on through every beat, every scene, and every act through the entire play. It is the ever changing flow of the character's inner action in which every actor must swim. If an actor wants to execute these actions effectively, he'll have to know, articulate, and play with the entire flow even if that seems a daunting assignment. This is the hard and close work that defines the technique of inner action. To balk because it is "difficult" is to believe that the actor can succeed without that level of craftsmanship. To balk at mastering intentions because you think the actor can't stop to think about the next action is to misunderstand the purpose of rehearsal.

"You want me to articulate every action in every beat? Nobody ever does that!" "Really?" "It'll be too much to think about. I have to go up there and remember lines and business and blocking and you want me to remember this stuff too? Forget it!" These perceptions have persuaded some to in effect reject mastery of the craft.

Anxieties About Remembering

The actor should never worry about remembering "this stuff" when he gets up there. I want the actors to think about inner action night and day throughout their lives *except* while performing. I want them to read every available script to discover the flow of actions, to look at every movie and television play from the point of view of inner action, and to determine the inner action in every personal encounter. Clarify personal objectives in your life. Decide to know the flow of actions in every scene. Explore those actions and the many ways of doing any one action as fully as possible in rehearsal. Discover the best, most vivid, and interesting ways to develop those actions by playing with them before the performance. Get to know the interplay of actions the way a painter gets to know the interplay of colors. The result will be that the actor's entire being will know what to do in performance without trying to think about actions or to remember them. Actors know they are in trouble when they have to try to remember lines. Lines should come fluently, almost automatically. It is precisely the same with the flow of actions.

I compare the phenomenon of "learning so you can forget" to the task of a professional downhill skier. If she is to achieve a world-class stature, she must master the knife-edge between annihilation and loitering. She can follow that fine line only when her skiing skills are at their peak, when she knows the slopes like her own face and better. Only then can she expect to enter a world-class challenge because she knows that her concentration will be flawless, that she won't distract herself worrying about what to do next. Her total being will just know.

Like the downhill skier, the audience ought perceive the actor's performance as something ordinary mortals cannot do. Her work ought seem as impossible and as easy as the flight of a trapeze artist. And that is something you cannot do if you worry about the next move. You know the next move, that next line, that next action because you rehearse. And like an acrobat or the downhill skier, the true master actor has rehearsed the performance until his entire being knows every moment in every limb and brain cell. He has enabled himself to adjust instantly to the slightest surprise without distracting himself from his purpose.

Everyone possesses skills they know so well that they don't have to think about while doing them. It's like walking, the process of falling forward and catching ourselves. We never have to think about falling and catching ourselves even when we're going over rough ground or down slippery slopes. Instinctively we know what to do. Our conscious mind does little to keep us walking. Our attention may wander through other realms while our feet test the toughest terrain. We can do this because we learned to walk so well we no longer have to think about it. We should design the rehearsal process to take actors to the point where they "don't have to think about doing it." The process should include a mastery of external movement and the entire process of clarifying, articulating, and mastering the inner actions. This is not for lazy people and for some performances it is a task that could take months of preparatory work. Nevertheless, the best actors on stage or film are doing this work and their process and their success are transforming the art of acting. They have trained themselves to master the techniques of inner action, the most important contribution of the Stanislavski heritage.

One Inner Action Can Be Performed in Infinite Ways

I can sense objections. "You are prescribing a rehearsal process that is tedious and boring." Quite the opposite. I am talking about a rehearsal process that is exciting and always challenging. Identifying and articulating the most appropriate inner action is not the end of the actor's work. As I stated earlier, the actor also should explore some of the infinite ways to perform every inner action.[11]

In the scene on the road to Padua, Petruchio says it's a wonderful moon up there and Kate says no, that's the sun. And he says OK, now we go home—coercing her. Or is he courting or, playing with her? Let's say he is coercing her: "If you don't agree with me, we are going to turn back and go home." Is he like a child who says, "If I can't be captain I'll take my football and go home?" How many ways are there to show that? Sulkily, with a long and ugly face: "I'll take my football and go home." Or is his coercing really playful? How about a joking, self-deprecating coercion: "I'll take my football and go home!" Another actor may choose an angry, mean-spirited coercion. All four ways are different. And there are an infinite number of other ways.

Knowing that there are so many possibilities for playing an action opens the actor to his own creativity. Our first choice does not have to be our last. Anger, for example, is often a quicksand for untutored actors who are tempted to unleash a blatant and unbridled expression of anger. Thus, if an actor playing Petruchio on the road to Padua decides that he is angry, he may lash out, attempting to coerce Kate with open anger, a mistaken choice. To decide Petruchio is angry may be appropriate, but to show the anger—to not hide it—wouldn't work. A brutal expression of anger is too unsophisticated for Petruchio. Let him play with anger, feel it, but hide or deny it to give the performance an edge that might worry the lady and prompt her concession.

The point I have been trying to make in this chapter is that the technique of inner action provides performers and others working with text a powerful process for preparing that text for performance. Before finally choosing an inner action appropriate to the circumstances of the script, we must do the following:

- Stay open to new possible actions even late in the rehearsal process. We should avoid locking our choice into the first action that comes to mind. There is a common tendency for people to make a first, intuitive choice that is commonplace and ordinary. A nice trick is to ask what the "opposite" choice might be, thereby exercising the imagination to new possibilities.
- Choose vibrant, colorful, and challenging actions. Explaining, trying, and showing are bland. We should ask ourselves why our character wants to show or explain. What is the character trying to accomplish by explaining? Is he actually trying to survive or to defend himself?
- Establish a relationship with the actions of fellow actors. Are the actions played by each actor in conflict with one another? Are the characters allies? We should always consider our choice of action in relation to the actions played by others in

the scene. Inner actions define the relationships between characters.

- Ensure that the actions chosen are *character* actions. Assuming that the actions are not the personal concerns of the actor, are the actions chosen director's or playwright's objectives, or are they character actions? Shakespeare may have wanted to explore how the sins of kings corrupt the state when he wrote the play, but *Hamlet's* action is not *to explore.* A director might want to update the script, a motive that could lead to new ideas about character actions but it is not an action for actors to play.

The Actor's Responsibilities 3

The Dark Side of Inner Action

*T*here is a negative aspect to using the technique of inner action: Actors blindly driven by an untempered passion to perform the character's inner action will trespass upon the work of fellow actors. Robert Benedetti in his essay "On Acting" says, "Too often actors arm themselves with an objective and then beat their partner to death with it; they try to make their action unilateral and fail to realize that action is always reciprocal. . . . they are trying to maintain complete control of the scene."[12] This is an important consideration.

Every actor has a responsibility to collaborate with the others in a scene so they don't trample each other's work. And to collaborate is an actor's inner action. As Robert Benedetti states, "The objective is best thought of as a desired change in the partner. . . . Defined in this way, the objective ensures contact between the characters so that the transaction of the scene that carries the dramatic action is most likely to occur."[13]

It is obvious, for example, that Romeo cannot so overwhelm Juliet with his desire to win her that the actress cannot play her actions. If the actor playing Romeo were so driven in the balcony scene that he would do his untempered anything to get her, he could easily inhibit her playing. Ignoring another actor's action is the potential dark side of the technique of inner action. Some actors become so enthusiastic about fighting for their actions they become oblivious to their responsibility to fellow players. We cannot overwhelm fellow actors with a runaway determination to do our own work.

The old stage dictum to listen has merit in this connection but it is really insufficient. The actor also has to see, to sense, and to comprehend what is going on and then *reciprocate*. With this notion of reciprocating we come to a crucial aspect of the technique of inner action that I call collaborative responding.

The Bright Side of Inner Action

I have gone to some lengths to impress on you that an *actor's* personal inner actions—like trying to impress the audience—are a problem. I am now going to alter my tack and examine a type of actor's inner action that must happen constantly in every performance. Collaborative responding is really an inter–inner action with fellow actors and audiences. Actors have an artistic obligation to respond to their colleagues on stage. Indeed, responding is so important that it becomes the primary inner action in many kinds of improvisational performance.

Let's go back to that scene in *King Lear* where the king is trying to charm his daughters. Let's suppose that, suddenly and surprisingly, in this performance the actress playing Regan lets out a squeal of surprise. Who knows why? Maybe rainwater dripped onto the back of her neck. What does the actor playing Lear do? Ignore it? No. He incorporates his response to her surprise into his performance. The rule is to accept everything that happens as a resource. Our challenge as actors is to go with our spontaneous response to that resource. From this perspective there are no mistakes—only opportunities. Ignore nothing. Regan snags her gown? An opportunity for the charming father. At the same time, I repeat that we must respect everything the director decided and rehearsed because performing what was practiced in rehearsal does not imply performing mechanically. Wonderful things happen when the actors take the risk of responding spontaneously. Their work jumps into life and the audience senses that vibrancy. Recall the experience of Hira Panth, the Bharatanatyam dancer, who freed herself with a newfound spontaneity that emerged with her inner action *to woo*. Spontaneous responding is a subtle exterior manifestation of inner life. It does not change the director's decisions.

Note that we're not talking about *reacting,* a word that suggests an impulsive, perhaps inappropriate opposition or reversing activity. *Responding collaboratively* suggests replying or answering or playing in a cooperative way. It is an objective that requires a profound respect for the work of fellow performers.

The rewarding, if uncanny, part is that, if risked, the true spontaneous and collaborative response will always be appropriate, full of life, and pregnant with surprise. This is the performance plane where intuitive acting *is* appropriate. When the actor risks spontaneous and collaborative responses—while respecting and doing everything that has been rehearsed—theater comes alive. It is at these moments that the hairs rise on the back of the audience's necks. These are the moments of magic. But how does this spontaneous moment relate to the technique of inner action?

Mastering the technique of inner action develops confidence and authority that allow actors to respond to one another and also to audiences and any other element that impinges on the performance. It is commonplace for directors to exhort actors "to go with your impulses," which is meant to encourage actors to respond to one another. Responding collaboratively allows actors to execute the text and the decisions honed by rehearsals and still go with their impulses with confidence. There is a nice paradox here: we earn the freedom to express our responses only by respecting everything we learned meticulously in the rehearsal process. The actor who incorporates into his performance his response to Regan's surprise at the ice water dripping onto her neck is not doing something difficult, unusual, or contrary to direction. He is doing what actors are supposed to do.

Think of it this way: Responding to fellow performers, even to audiences, is an actor's responsibility that must accompany the flow of character actions. The continual interplay of an actor's response and a character's inner action defines the psychologically healthy performance. The vital interplay of character action and actor response also makes for the necessarily fluid texture of performance. Spontaneous response makes performance live. Without responding, the actor's work becomes wooden, tedious, insipid, lifeless—nothing but words uttered and movements executed.

When Hira Panth incorporated inner actions into her dance wooing Krishna, her audience responded to the wooing and Hira responded in turn to the audience, and the two—performer and audience—joined in an electrifying response-reaction flow. The experience becomes interactive. The audience ceases to be passive. The same things happen between players on stage.

Without the response-reaction flow between and among the players you have mere robot behavior. You might as well put machines on that stage. To play with a partner is to respond to that partner, to risk your own spontaneous response. And I will emphasize again that all of this is done without changing the objectives and moves and timing that were set with the director in rehearsal.

Play Brings Performance to Life

There are two principles of collaborative responding that are important to know. The first principle is that when actors respond collaboratively to one another, they begin to play with one another. The second principle is that the truly spontaneous response will always be appropriate. I'll repeat that. The truly spontaneous response is *always* appropriate, without qualification. And how do you know it was appropriate? What is the test? Exhilaration. If the actors feel exhilarated by the interaction rather than bored or self-conscious, the response was spontaneous. We must risk the spontaneous response because it is only by responding to the partner's performance that a performer earns the title of player. Collaborative responding provides the mechanism for play between actors.

All responses between actors on stage ought be essentially playful even when the script calls for something grim or solemn. In actuality the actors are only playing with each other, so the interaction among them must be spontaneous even when their activity is somber.

> Creative work is play; it is free speculation using the materials of one's chosen form. The creative mind plays with the objects it loves. Artists play with color and space. Musicians play with sound and silence. Eros plays with lovers. Gods play with the universe. Children play with everything they can get their hands on.[14]

Without play, there are no surprises or joy in the performance, just ennui for the audiences and angst for the actors. If Katherine should suddenly respond to Petruchio with an unaccustomed dark fury when he expects a lighter touch characteristic of their rehearsals, he can't just ignore her. He must respond to her in a way that respects her choice. He must risk his spontaneous response and deal with her emotional state respectfully even if he is surprised and unprepared. This fluid interplay of responses is one of the determinants of how the actor plays the inner action of the moment.

Pushing this hypothetical moment in *The Taming of the Shrew* a bit more, let's imagine that we are in performance and that Petruchio's objective or inner action in their first scene together is *to win* Katherine. How does he set out *to woo*? Roughly? Charmingly? Wittily? Lovingly? All of these? Perhaps her response has been characterized all along by a sharp-edged but essentially good-humored response, but today for some reason her response darkens. That darkening requires a different response from the actor playing Petruchio. He suddenly finds that he must play with his partner in a different way. He must respond to her exceptionally darkened mood. He must see it as a resource that will help them keep their performance alive and do all the things that he has rehearsed—saying lines without alteration, doing the blocking and business decreed by the director, and staying with his rehearsed objectives. Actors who perform precisely as directed from night to night in a responsive mode guarantee truly living and animated theater experiences. Of course, when I speak of *playing* I do not mean *goofing*. The latter is a protective behavior that is always inappropriate unless the character is written as a goofer. I discuss this problem below.

Inner Action and Self: To Risk, Surrender, and Accept

To respond authentically we have to learn to surrender both to our *own* total being and to external input. We have to make ourselves vulnerable to ourselves. We have to find the willingness to express everything that is us, both the negative and the positive. We have to come to see that everything about us is a resource, including those aspects of ourselves that we wish we could get rid of or adjust. Total acceptance is the only way we can express ourselves authentically.

How do we achieve this surrender? By letting go of our obsessions with the "bad parts" and not by trying to surrender; there is no way we can try to surrender. If we don't surrender we will have no way to respond spontaneously. If we wish to become successful performing artists we have no choice but to accept ourselves totally, abandoning our defenses. Does Hamlet have to be broad shouldered and small waisted, wear flowing locks, and have the athletic ability of Douglas Fairbanks, Jr. How about a short, paunchy, balding Hamlet in his early fifties? Violations of tradition provide the opportunity for new explorations of the text with new resources.

Only by totally accepting herself will the actor risk using that self in the charged atmosphere of performance. What can we do that makes this surrender to our inner reality possible? First, we have to understand that we have no choice. We have to surrender and risk because there is no way to dissemble, fake, feign, or pretend and make it work. If we dissemble we will broadcast pretense. The basic problem is that faking is probably the wrong inner action for the character anyway!

Daniel Goleman, reporting on studies of the interplay of moods between human beings, quotes Carl Jung's comment that "Emotions are contagious."[15] Goleman goes on to say that new data collected by experimental psychologists shows that "moods are akin to social viruses, with some people having a natural ability to transmit them while others are more susceptible to contagion."[16] He could be talking about the dynamic between actors and audiences that so many actors know. Goleman goes on to quote Elaine Hatfield, a psychologist at the University of Hawaii: "Emotional contagion happens within milliseconds, so quick you can't control it and so subtly that you're not really aware it's going on."[17] John Cacciopo, a psychologist at Ohio State, says, "The more emotionally expressive people are, the more apt they are to transmit their moods to someone they talk with. Just seeing someone express an emotion can evoke that mood in you. This dance of moods goes on between people all the time."[18] And it is because of the communication of mood that audiences tend to think of acting as being focused on feeling rather than action.

The actor must not deceive himself about the communication of moods and feelings. Worrying about negative aspects of self will confuse our inner actions. We will communicate our concern and our audiences may applaud, but that applause does not mean we have done our best work. Applause is not a test of success. Audiences may unconsciously deny their real responses to a performance because those real feelings conflict with what they have been told they ought to feel. It may be they think they should be pleased though their true inner experience may be indifference, confusion, or alienation.

An audience may be attached in some way positively or negatively to a performer and suppress its real response because of a need to experience the performer as either successful or not.

Political ideas may affect our attitude toward the performer. We may suppress our real responses to the work. If I am an old buddy of the real Roy Cohn, I may not cheer Ron Leibman's prize-winning performance, but I might applaud because all around me applaud. Audience response is no reason for actors to fail to risk total acceptance of self.

The best acting requires that the actor's inner reality and external expression are congruent. We muster the courage and take the risk to surrender because we have no other choice. When we risk that surrender to our inner reality we will express our own truth. As artists we can only pledge ourselves to suppress our fears and risk the truthful performance.

Fear weakens. It brings on the painful paralysis of self-consciousness, which smothers us if called upon to speak when we are unprepared to speak. The secret that releases us from this self-consciousness is to seek an inner action and focus exclusively on that action. For the actor who plays her character's action and surrenders to the risks of responding spontaneously, there will be no blight of self-consciousness and no attention directed to self. Release the self. Direct attention to action. This is what Yeats meant when he imagined the dancer becoming the dance. Performers define the performance when they concentrate on appropriate inner actions.

There is nothing new and no mystery about freeing oneself with action. The unself-conscious state happens all the time. It is, hopefully, the most common experience in our lives, happening when we concentrate on the food shopping or house cleaning or talking with a friend. We aren't judging ourselves, watching ourselves, or distracting ourselves. We are just doing the job. We are free of the pressure to perform.

In those moments of daily life we define many actions, such as shopping or cleaning. We become the action. We become what shopping is. Through the action we become what we want to be. We just say "I'm shopping." Think of *shopping* here as a gerund— a noun—as well as a verb, since both verb and noun exist in the construction. In our language and in our poetry, when we are profoundly involved with action, we bring being and action together. There are moments in life when it is through action that we can best describe to ourselves what we *are*. To do that we concentrate ourselves on the action. We then become congruent, focused, and capable of spontaneity.

Stephen Nachmanovitch describes an experience in his book *Free Play* in which he passes an office that had been a music practice room with a sign on the door that read, "This Is No Longer a Practice Room." Underneath somebody scribbled, "Now It's Perfect!" He goes on to make the point that practice is not dreary repetition designed to make us perfect.

> . . . If we split practice from the real thing, . . . which is the actualization of the complete person who is already there . . . [nothing] will be very real . . . The most frustrating, agonizing part of creative work, and the one we grapple with everyday in practice, is our encounter with the gap between what we feel and what we can express.[19]

If we cannot achieve inner harmony, if there is a "gap between what we feel and what we can express," we need help. Persistent self-consciousness shows us to be in a state of disharmony with ourselves. Disharmony produces anxiety and depression and causes us to lose the spontaneity required for healthy living. Fear will overwhelm us. We will find it impossible to surrender and take the risk to pursue our actions responsively and playfully.

Spontaneity and Inner Action 4

S pontaneous, ad hoc performance has always been a part of theater. It was practiced in the Greek and Roman comic traditions. The Italian *commedia dell'arte* was based on it. Spontaneity in performance is the hallmark of the best kind of acting. Americans call it "improvisation" suggesting unscripted, live performance in which an entire sketch, scene, or play is created on the spot before the audience's very eyes. I choose to use the term *spontaneity* because its meaning more easily extends to include meticulously rehearsed and scripted as well as ad hoc performances.

As we proceed, keep in mind that *collaborative responding* is an actor's objective. So are surrendering and wanting to succeed, to train, to get cast, to follow instructions, to perform and more. The difference is that *responding* is an appropriate actor's action that the actor will play simultaneously with any character action the actor is playing. It is this combination of inner actions working together simultaneously during the performance that enlivens the work with inimitable spontaneous behavior.

Others have recognized that performers can harden themselves with a flock of unconscious actor actions that are irrelevant to the character. In 1964, Victor Manukov, a director at the Moscow Art Theater explicitly made the point that the character's objective is not the only objective the actor works with.[20] He used the example of a soccer player's objectives. Like actors, soccer players have objectives beyond the immediate concerns of the game or "script." They want *to score* as much as possible. They want *to win*. They want *to defend* the team's record. They want *to win* the World Cup. They want *to spread* soccer all over the world. But the player isn't thinking about any of these things. Yet he goes "straight toward them every second of the game. . . . He appraises the situation. He senses the people around him. He moves to or from the ball. All his [activities] are prompt and logical." Metaobjectives inform the players' preparation for performance but, except for the readiness to respond, they are put aside during performance.

Risking: A Closer Look

Since risking is essential to spontaneous performance, I would insist that we add to the list of actor's metaobjectives the realization that we must decide *to risk*. Risking in the sense I am using it is different from the risks we take when we parachute from bridges or decide to take a plunge in the stock market. It is not a risk to life or to material well-being; it is a subtler and, for some, a more difficult risk. It is the risk to self-image, to the psychological armor that protects our image of ourselves from the aggressions of the world. Though this risk does not endanger us physically or financially, risking self-image brings the same thrills, sense of danger, and exhilaration available to the downhill skier or the rock climber. The characteristics of actors ready to risk are emotional maturity, humility, and a self-deprecating sense of humor.

The performer who accepts all of her resources—whether negative or positive—cultivates the readiness to risk self-image. The most interesting performers are not the prettiest but the ones who have learned to accept their entire inheritance and use it as fully as possible. In this sense handicaps become gifts and mistakes become opportunities. In his chapter "The Power of Mistakes," Nachmanovitch says, "If the oyster had hands, there would be no pearl. Because the oyster is forced to live with the irritation for an extended period, the pearl comes into being. . . . [The value of mistakes is that they are] the raw material of learning."[21]

The experience of a woman I'll call Rebecca provides a good example of a person whose talents were freed because she learned to set aside her armor and *to risk* her inner resources. When I first met her, Rebecca was a young woman with no previous acting experience who, after much urging from a friend, had relctantly auditioned for and been cast in a campus production. Her performance turned out to be a brilliant success. After this, Rebecca, like many other undergraduates who discover hidden talent in a college production, decided to become an actress. When she signed up for a scene study class, however, it turned out to be difficult and frustrating for Rebecca and for everyone who had to work with her. She showed persistence, though, and her teacher eventually suggested that she join my improvisation workshop.

From the beginning of the workshop, Rebecca experienced a painful self-consciousness whenever she became the focus of the work. For whatever reasons, she monitored every move she made, keeping to a limited repertory of self-approved behaviors. Everything she did was wooden and unresponsive. Unlike her first experience on stage when she had abandoned herself to the performance, she would almost paralyze herself in the workshop with concern about her behavior. Rebecca couldn't take a risk; there was no life in her work, no surprises. She had become a slave to the need to get it right. She had armored herself against error, against criticism. She had lost the ability *to choose* to risk. She was locked into the need to always "get it right."

Happily, Rebecca's determination to get it right also made her a careful observer of the other participants in the workshop. Before long, she saw that the actors whose work was most interesting were the ones who freed themselves to take the most risks. She observed how they put aside their armor by focusing on the inner actions of the characters they created.

After Rebecca made the choice to set aside her own psychological armor and take a risk on spontaneous, unmonitored behavior, her own work changed quickly. As she learned to focus exclusively on the inner actions of her characters, each performance came alive. She felt the exhilaration of spontaneity. Rebecca proved she had courage and talent. She went on to become a successful professional and, years later, a regular on a nationally broadcast situation comedy.

However, some of the armor we have molded for our psyches is a good thing and we would be foolish to discard it. I am not exhorting actors to lose the choice of shielding themselves, to abandon caution and self-protection. I have seen tightly armored people come into workshop, experience the freedom that comes with risking, and decide that having defenses is inappropriate and that they could live without them. It didn't take long until they found pain and disillusionment. The wise performer will keep a defensive armor available, choosing vulnerability only when vulnerability is appropriate and maintaining guardedness, caution, and a clear-eyed skepticism when caution is appropriate. The often-disregarded task of the teacher or director is to guarantee the safety of the workshop or rehearsal space. We should make it a psychological womb where the actor can find the courage to experiment with every resource, even those viewed as deficits. Problems with our armor occur only when we *lose* the choice to put aside that protection. The consequence of that loss of choice is to choke off the flow of our spontaneous responses. This flow of authentic responses, rooted in the flow of inner action, creates the finest, most exhilarating performances. The development of our spontaneity leads us to an awareness of that fact.

The actor who risks being spontaneous knows he must never try to please or impress in performance. If in rehearsal or performance we feel inappropriately manipulated or controlled or deceived, the appropriate spontaneous response is to stop responding. Armoring can be the actor's best response. Just as we will accept no manipulating or controlling from others, we must learn to put aside those tendencies in ourself. The need to control our talent with sharply honed technique is evident. Inner actions like controlling other people or manipulating them cause problems for fellow actors.

Seeking Self-Acceptance, Avoiding Imitation

Accepting ourselves and whatever we have to work with is the beginning of magic. With acceptance comes new strength, which brings forward a deeply enriched sense of humor and maturity. Yet it really isn't surprising that many would-be performers who discover some talent in themselves or some delight in the act of performing try to imitate a model—a star—they find particularly attractive. Of course, that is precisely the wrong thing to do. We neither need nor want a second Paul Newman or Meryl Streep. We want you. The most successful performers have succeeded precisely because they had the courage to cultivate the expression of all of their own authentic inheritance, both the pluses and the minuses. They have taken the risk to invest in themselves and found unlimited veins of gold. We are all offered the same cosmic gift.

The qualities that make a star are always unique to that person. It may be an act of faith, but for me every healthy, functioning human being has qualities to develop, to encourage, and to risk using, qualities that will lead to success if developed. Our audiences want actors who are authentic, integrated human beings who need to imitate no one; actors who will take the risk those audiences dare not take themselves. To succeed as person and performer, the actor must eventually come to feel the need to grow and mature, to become a discoverer of a personal and unique identity that necessarily includes negative and positive elements. Only then will the actor be ready to risk dropping the protective mechanisms and denials that function automatically, the tactics that bring a false sense of security to those moments when we face a challenge to our self-image.

For example, a problem that still haunts some performers, especially New Yorkers, is the regional accent. Someone probably tells them their accent is bad and unsophisticated and marks them as inferior. They learn to dislike the way they speak and feel there is something wrong with themselves. Not so. We have to understand that our accents are a resource despite the prejudice against them. The challenge for the performer is not to abandon a regional heritage but to develop other accents. Even better, actors should develop the skill of mastering accents. The accents of a skilled actor are like a closet of costumes ready for whatever occasion. None of them are inherently bad.

What happens when we take the risk to use those aspects of ourselves that bother us—when we stop trying to change that squeaky voice into a sultry baritone, when we stop hiding our faces with hair, when we stop trying to hide our baldness? When we accept ourselves, we allow audiences to identify with us. When we risk and make ourselves vulnerable, others see us daring to live authentically and recognize the courage of that risk. The audience becomes our friend.

The Dynamics of Flowing Action

The spontaneous response is always appropriate. It may not be the best choice but spontaneous responses—if truly spontaneous—are always appropriate even when we use mistakes as resources. Spontaneity always feels good. If the response is not spontaneous it will generate discomfort or self-consciousness. Consider pedestrians on a crowded sidewalk in a major city at lunchtime. Not only are they moving in two directions, they come from all sides: from building entrances, from across the street, from automobiles at the curb. They come along singly and in groups. They move at all speeds. Some run. Some barely move. The extraordinary thing is how few collisions occur. Even when they divide their concentration between walking and window shopping or talking or sightseeing, they manage to avoid each other. And if they don't? If there is a mistake? A collision? They respond, apologize, and move on—and the flow continues unabated. The whole scene demonstrates improvisational performance. People generally rely on their spontaneous responses in situations like that. We risk those responses because it works. Performers must learn to develop that same confidence in performance. Like the walkers on the city sidewalk, our performance risks seem less risky as confidence in our inner resources grows. And when we finally learn our true worth, the sense of risk disappears. We begin to play. We begin to think we can negotiate busy sidewalks wearing rollerblades.

A flow of spontaneous activity occurs between performers when each acts in response to the other. Every night the two actors playing Hamlet and his mother enact her bedroom scene with a slightly different texture without changing the way they rehearsed it. The performances keep changing but the audience doesn't know it keeps changing. People only know they have seen a fresh and vivid sequence of acting. The only people who know the performance texture differs in each performance and stays full of surprises are the stage manager and some technicians whose task it is to watch it every night. If we asked the stage manager if the two actors change their inner actions from performance to performance, we'd probably learn that they do not. The inner actions stay but in some subtle way the expression of them changes. Tonight's grumpiness or sniffles, perhaps caused by something totally unrelated to the partner or the play, generates a surprising response that itself generates a surprising response. They have created a spontaneous, ever-changing texture rooted in inner action.

There are some consistent characteristics of this flow. Each individual act will always seem to have been appropriate—the characteristic of spontaneity. Players in a flow will report that it was as though they had been reading each other's thoughts. A flow will strengthen the willingness of partners to trust and collaborate. The experience of a flow will leave the participants with a feeling of exhilaration, and that feeling is the touchstone of the process. They can judge their experience by the degree of elation or joy they feel when it ends. The opposite is also true: if at the end of an interaction there are negative feelings like depression, self-consciousness, frustration, awkwardness, or discomfort, everybody concerned will know there has been no spontaneous flow of collaborative responding. Faking an improvisation is disconcerting and annoying to watch. A truly spontaneous flow entertains and fascinates onlookers.

An example of this behavioral fluency that we have all experienced is infectious laughter. Two people talking together find themselves laughing out of control. That laughter could have begun with some innocuous, even unfunny matter. As we respond to the laughter of the other, the act of laughing and the laughing response take over. An irresistible flow of laughter emerges, captivating both people in its seemingly self-generated way. The laughing response of one to the other created a flow. Soon, even onlookers are caught up in the flow of laughter. A flow of responses can be verbal or nonverbal. We are often witnesses to a situation between two people where the exchange of witticisms seems astonishingly quick and apt. They are on a roll together, a nice description of the uninterrupted quality of responses.

Frequently, a flow will have blinding speed. Where does that speed come from? Intelligence, yes, but many highly intelligent people seem incapable of it. Rapidity comes from a willingness to heed what is happening and then to risk an unedited inner response. The flow does not happen if an actor just wants to prove how witty he is. We really have but one choice: to trust our native wit and let it flow in response.

The flow of the responses facilitates the responding. Think of trying to get a flywheel started. It requires effort and energy to get it going, but once the wheel is flying it needs little to keep it going. Interrupt the flow of responses and you lose the response momentum and fluency ends. We have to exert extra energy to begin the flow again. When one actor stops responding, the other actor is left with no place to go and nothing to respond to. If one performer senses that a partner has lost contact, that the partner is no longer responding with full concentration, or that something else has caught the partner's attention, spontaneity will fail. The fluidity of action depends on the total concentration of each partner on the exchange of responses. Improvisational musicians understand this well. It is an important jazz tradition and should be part of the tradition of the actor as well.

An Exercise in the Response-Reaction Flow

Try the following nonverbal exercise with a friend. Read the directions before you try the experiment and make sure you understand the instructions thoroughly. Take appropriate pauses. Allow yourself the freedom of discovery.

1. All of the movements in this exercise should be kept abstract; that is, avoid doing movements that are content laden like the hand signal for stopping or familiar signs like brushing your teeth.
2. Stand facing your partner.
3. Extend your right hands palm up so they are side by side.
4. Watch your partner's hand and not your hand.
5. Look for normal involuntary movement in your partner's hand. Unless your partner is in rigor mortis, you will observe some movement.
6. Respond to that movement with movement in your hand. Give as much as you saw or more. Just let it happen.
7. Play until a flow develops but never decide what to do. Just respond. Did you generate a flow? If so, then stop.
8. Let this responding with your hands become a nonverbal conversation using abstract movement. One of you should make an abstract hand movement and stop.
9. The other partner should now move her hand in response to that movement and then stop.
10. Continue this process of response using abstract gestures only. Don't think about your reply—just risk a movement.
11. Continue using both hands.
12. Now enter your partner's space and involve more of your body. Respond as long as the dynamic between you holds your interest and energizes you. A natural stopping time will come. You will both know when it is over.

The first time you do this you might feel awkward. If so, then start again. You will develop fluency and flow as you perfect the exercise. You may even come to a point where you sense the very instant that you should stop together. Yet each time you do the exercise it will change and you will invent a new choreography.

You are engaging in free play—improvisational, collaborative, and spontaneous performance.

One person can do the same exercise alone, using one hand to respond to the other, even one hand to one foot if you're sufficiently flexible. Extend the play in an imaginative way. Let the two hands be birds engaged in freewheeling aerobatics in the space around your body. See how quickly the response of one hand's actions to the other hand's actions achieves free play. In everyday life it is this flow of responses that makes interactions between people satisfying, amusing, and intimate.

On the highway in crowded traffic, the good driver is the one whose responses are tuned in to the actions of other drivers. Drivers too timid to respond to traffic or drivers who try aggressively to dominate traffic are out of harmony and will disturb others. The same dynamic is true of lovers. People who think of physical intimacy only in terms of rubbing their physical apparatus are—literally—out of touch. Lovers who act in response to one another will satisfy and bring joy to each other. The lover who insists on controlling the interactions becomes a problem for the partner, leaving passivity as an unsatisfactory alternative. Whenever a partner chooses either passivity or domination, mutual spontaneity ends.

Once the actor develops a flow of responses, the work seems effortless. Even apparent blunders, stumbling, and mischance become part of the flow if partners concentrate, risk, and have the skills to use everything they are given. The consequence of risking spontaneity is that everything we do in the flow of responses is appropriate. And both actor and audience know it.

People unable to respond usually have an agenda and a narrow vocabulary of action that they want or need to impose on partners. In free-movement exercises, people not yet ready to risk truly free movement will substitute moves they know like dance steps; males new to this work often begin nonverbal improvisations by miming a fight. The problem is that these studied movements have a restricted vocabulary that limit and block the responses of the partner. That is why I ask you to do the hand dancing exercise with abstract movement. And restricted vocabularies often lead to control and passivity. Everyone must be fully active; passivity is never an option. The passive partner may generate fear in his partner—fear that he is indifferent or unconcerned—which discourages risk and spontaneous responses.

A flow of spontaneous action requires the actor to be open to use anything that comes his way, short of genuine aggression or physical attack. Furthermore (and don't be confused by this), a flow of action requires each person to alternate continually between assertive and receptive behavior: giving and receiving, acting and taking in. This pattern is characteristic of the flow. It is the pulse beat and rhythm of spontaneous activity.

Collaboration develops in an environment of trust, and trust itself expands and deepens with collaboration. No one controls anyone else—everyone gives, everyone takes, everyone uses what they get, everyone risks what they have to offer. We have the power to act and attend to the responses coming at us simultaneously. The actor's task is to cultivate that ability.

In his book *Flow*, the psychologist Mihaly Csikszentmihalyi makes a crucial point about this topic. He says that all human beings are subject to either psychic entropy, in which the individual allows unwanted information coming in from experience to block and frustrate objectives, or optimal experience, in which the individual learns to control her response to incoming experience so that unwanted information does not block us.[22] Performers collaborate to avoid unwanted information, feeding each other with responses that arise from the interaction to create a living performance. And performance must live. Without that flow of responses between performers and audiences, the performance dies, lacking freshness and that necessary feeling of "the first time."

Csikszentmihalyi writes from the perspective of an experimental psychologist when he says that happiness is simply a byproduct of being concentrated on action in which a flow of responses develops. This prescription is precisely the same as Stanislavski's insight about the actor's work with inner action decades earlier. If we learn to manage this process with skill, the indirect result is the reward of happiness, contentment, and exhilaration.

Collaboration: Struggling Together with Generosity

Performers collaborate rather than compete. Two improvisors begin an exercise designed to explore character relationships. One decides without informing his partner that the best approach to the exercise should be verbal. The other privately decides to take a nonverbal approach. The first attempts a shower of words ignored by the second who, determined to communicate only through body language, strives thereby to get the other to do the same. The first, frustrated by the second (who has become a competitor) tries even harder to control their interaction with words. These two combatants cannot improvise because they are not collaborators. They are not engaged in character exploration. They are not helping each other. Neither sees nor hears the other. Both have decided what to do and have focused on that. They are combatants following predetermined agendas or strategies.

Combatants proceed without considering or attending to the other party. They are not collaborative. They cannot achieve spontaneity. They will frustrate each other and bore anybody who has to watch them. They have not yet learned that the performer must accept and work with responses, with what they get from their partner, a rule every improvisational performer accepts as canon law.

The Willingness to Explore, Test and Evaluate

What is this subtle dynamic of giving and getting "gifts"? What is the relationship between giving and getting, assertiveness and passivity? These two modes of being operate like a constantly changing positive-negative switch. When the switch is at one pole, we attend to the gift from our partner. When the switch is at the other pole, we respond by giving a gift. This exchange can happen with blinding speed. Having heard, felt, or seen the gift of a response, our unedited self responds and drives the interaction, freeing the performers from trying to "take it somewhere." To collaborate within that flow is to ensure that we are fully and wholly concentrated on the individual moment that is, after all, the only reality.

Distinguishing Impetuosity and Spontaneity

There are risks worth taking and there are foolish risks. If you wish to see straight down over the edge of the roof of a forty-story building it would be foolish to trot out onto that unguarded edge and stand with your toes tickling space. Do it and you'll experience a fear and trembling for your life. On the other hand, were you to lie flat on that roof, you could safely place your entire head and even shoulders out beyond the edge with no risk to life and get as good a view. There are smart risks and foolish risks.

An Olympic diver—a performer—stands on the ten-meter board thirty-three feet above water that on impact can be as hard as concrete. He stands with eyes closed in deepening concentration, probably seeing in his mind's eye the whole sequence of events from the time movement begins until entering the water. Most of us would be foolish to do what he is doing. The risks are obvious. However, for this diver the risks are minimal because he knows what he is doing. If this is truly a gold medal dive, everything the diver does in those fleeting instants between leaping from the tower and slipping into the water will be virtually perfect. It will be a series of both spontaneous and well-rehearsed moves arising naturally one after the other without him needing to stop to think, judge, or consider the next move.

To stand tiptoe at the edge of the roof is impetuous. To stand at the edge of the ten-meter board and follow through into the dive requires a string of spontaneous behaviors from that trained diver. Consider the definitions of *spontaneity* and *impetuosity*. Generally, I think English-speaking people tend to regard them as synonymous. The thesaurus in my computer does. *The Oxford English Dictionary* is more precise and describes *impetuous* as "acting with rash energy" and *spontaneity* as naturalness and acts arising from voluntary reasons. *Webster's Deluxe Unabridged Desk Dictionary* lists synonyms of *impetuous* as "rushing, hasty, precipitate, impulsive, vehement, rash, fiery, fierce, passionate," and "acting suddenly with little thought; rash, impulsive." *Webster's* defines *spontaneous* as "acting in accordance with or resulting from natural feeling, temperament, or disposition, or from a native internal proneness, readiness or tendency without compulsion, constraint, or premeditation." *Impulsive* and *spontaneous* are not synonyms except in loose, colloquial usage. These are descriptions of contrasting behaviors—one negative, the other positive, one inappropriate, the other appropriate.

Spontaneous behavior occurs within the flow and is *always* appropriate. Impetuous behavior happens outside of the response-reaction flow. It does not spring responsively from the actions that have gone before. It does not come from a "native" knowledge of what to do next. It is only accidentally appropriate. An impetuous act comes from an anxiety about not knowing what to do next and is heedless and reckless.

When performers wonder what to do next, tension develops, which leads them to act impetuously. This can happen because of an unwillingness to risk or a failure of concentration. What distracts the performer? a poor self-image? Learn to accept all of your resources. If you are afraid, take a risk. If you have a need to control, surrender. Ultimately, however, we solve the problem of failed concentration by finding and pursuing the flow of inner action.

Spontaneity is the expression of true freedom. The root of the word is in the Latin *sponte,* "of free will," which is unrelated to the Latin source of impetuous, *impetere,* meaning "to rush upon." The latter is more closely related to compulsion, control, or dominance than to freedom. How, then, can spontaneity arise from the fully rehearsed performer? How is this different from so-called "free" improvisation—the improvisation without a script? Fundamentally there is no difference. Free improvisation emerges from life knowledge, from the unconsciously well rehearsed life.

When we do not accept ourselves totally, we tend to shy away from spontaneous behavior and fear or distrust any responses we might make. We seek external authority or rigid formulas to reassure ourselves and end our anxiety. The failure of spontaneity results in the loss of inner authority and the ability to play. Those who cannot play are left with no choice but to goof.

The Problem of Performance Pressure

There is no similarity between authentic play and goofing or silly behavior. The latter is characterized by an essential stupidity that we feel in ourselves when we do it. Actors can fall into this trap when trying to play farce, thinking that the humor arises from goofish or stupid behavior when, in fact, the fun emerges from actors performing characters who are struggling monomaniacally to execute their inner actions.

The primary difference between goofing and play is self-consciousness and anxiety about the worth of "me." The goofer focuses on self: "How am I doing? What do they think of me? What shall I do next? Is this all right?" The paradox is that the more I try to protect me, show me off, or emphasize me, the more I achieve what I dread: the conviction that I am worth less than other human beings, which is a sad accomplishment.

But we do not inherit goofing and there is a way out. Play with the character's inner actions within the flow of responses. As we have seen over and over again in this study, everything comes back to that simple necessity. The goofer concentrates on "me." The player concentrates on actions in response to fellow players. The player is comfortable and easy. The goofer is uncomfortable and uneasy.

When we learn to prepare ourselves physically, emotionally, and intellectually for the moment the performance begins, we will move from feeling pressure to perform—which is natural—to the state of unself-conscious readiness before the performance begins. The secret lies in having a preparation that helps us to center ourselves and find our poise and stability. Effective preparation for performance makes our inner self like a perfectly spinning top with all forces equalized, unlike a wobbly top where the forces are unstable. We prepare to concentrate on the flow of inner action by bringing ourselves to a state of centered readiness.

We have to develop a routine of preparation that takes us from social concerns and worries about self to a state of readiness to act. Our minds must be cleared of anxieties, our bodies poised. Breathing, relaxation, physical warmup, and a review of what we want to accomplish are necessary. To develop a routine of physical and mental preparation that we repeat before every workshop, rehearsal, and performance effectively conditions us to surrender to the actions required by the performance rather than to the anxieties of performance pressure.

The actor who ignores preparation will become the victim of pressure and anxiety. People who undervalue full preparation find the quality of their work dismaying. They begin to feel inadequate to the task and, worse, they weaken their own self-image. They do the very thing they most dread. Succumbing to the anxieties of performance pressure leads to goofing rather than appropriate play. It is important to keep in mind that we do not have to be helpless corks tossed in the violent seas of our emotional states. We don't have to be victims caught up in anxieties. We have a choice. The better choice, the choice the performer must learn to make, is to surrender to the actor's responsibility, to execute the inner actions of the character.

A Historical 5
Sketch

Twenty-five Hundred Years Without a Technique of Inner Action

For centuries critics and theorists of performance have tried to write about real feeling on the stage with little success, often obfuscating the entire problem. There have been several hypotheses explaining how we express emotion and if indeed that expression is authentic. Some have said that actors do not feel the emotions they portray, and others have disagreed. Actors wanted to achieve the expression of emotional truth from the very beginning. Those who believed they really had to feel authentic emotional states always seem to have thought about the process of achieving that expression from the audience point of view, believing that their task was to somehow *be* or *become*—be angry, become confused. Few thought about the problem from the perspective of action, although they called themselves actors. Others gave up on that internal approach, believing that the expression of feeling was really only a technical problem involving external use of the actor's body. These two schools of thought persist today in spite of the development of the conscious technique of inner action from Stanislavski's insights in the first quarter of this century.

Plutarch, pondering the role of the actor in our lives, wondered, "Why take we delight in hearing those that represent the passions of men angry or sorrowful, and yet

cannot, without concern, behold those who are really so af-
fected?"[23] Aristotle told poets to be like actors for "They are most
. . . affecting . . . [and] we share the agitation of those who appear
to be truly agitated—the anger of those who appear to be truly
angry."[24] Plutarch also gives us the example of the Roman tragedian Aesop, who got so carried away playing Atreus's anger
about Thyestes's behavior that he struck out at one of his fellow
players and actually killed him.[25] This was very unprofessional
and uncollaborative and not very skillful. Of course, there is the
famous story about the Greek tragedian Polus told by Aulus
Gellius in his *Attic Nights*.[26] Polus was playing Sophocles's Electra
and had to carry an urn that was supposed to contain the ashes
of Orestes. Polus, giving his all to what we now call "affective
memory"—feeling any emotion on cue—took from the "tomb the
ashes and urn of his son, embraced them as if they were those of
Orestes, and filled the whole place, not with the appearance and
imitation of sorrow, but with genuine grief and unfeigned lamen-
tation." Some actors will do anything to achieve an authentic
expression of emotion.

These descriptions of the actor's work from the audience's
point of view always seem to have been concerned with feeling
and not with action. Few seem ever to have taken a clue from the
name *actor* and thought the issue might have to do with action.
Feeling or the absence of feeling was the concern of Denis
Diderot, the eighteenth-century encyclopedist, in *The Paradox of
Acting*, one of the earliest European attempts to theorize about
the problem. And later, the English critic William Archer replied
in *Masks or Faces* to Diderot but speaks from the same audience
perspective when he says that acting is a process of imitation and
that the actor "imitates the manners and passions of other
men."[27] Archer did use a verb—imitate—to describe the actor's
work, but it was probably unconscious and not even noticed by
Archer himself. In any event, *to imitate* manners is an *actor's*
objective and not a character objective, a distinction almost never
made by early commentators.

Many eminent figures in the history of twentieth-century theater have looked at the problem from the audience perspective as
well. Typically, they focus on the psychology of emotion to dissect
the way actors express emotion. They display little understanding
of what really happens in performance, thinking in the abstract
about the problem rather than closely observing the actor's work.
Edward Gordon Craig, for instance, in *The Actor and the Über-
Marionette* says, "Acting is not an art. . . . That which the actor gives

us . . . is a series of accidental confessions."[28] He is clearly saying what many today still believe: that there is no possibility of inner technique in the craft of the actor. Craig is still presented to theater history students as a major thinker in twentieth-century theater.

A hundred years ago we find Irving giving Macready's definition of action: "To fathom the depth of character, to trace its latent motives, to feel its fine quiverings of emotion, is to comprehend the thoughts that are hidden under words and thus possess one's self of the actual mind of the individual man."[29] This is very close. He is telling us to identify the given circumstances and the subtext. But that is not enough and not a very clear definition of *action*. He says that the actor needs to know the given circumstances, which is the necessary first step, but is he saying that "to possess one's self of the actual mind of the individual man" is to know and articulate his inner action? Perhaps, but I wish he had said so with a clearer emphasis.

One of the few precise examples of an actor aware of a character's inner action comes from Adelaide Ristori in "My Study of Lady Macbeth," where she writes that Lady Macbeth is "motivated only by her excessive ambition to reign with [Macbeth]."[30] "To reign" is an example of what Stanislavski decades later called the superobjective! She then goes on to list some of the given circumstances of the play and tells us how Lady Macbeth "used her affection for [Macbeth] as a means to satisfy her ambition." She says that Lady Macbeth took advantage of his fascination for her by "instilling into his mind the virus of crime." *To satisfy* and *to instill* are vivid and lucid actions offered by Ristori as subobjectives or tactics an actor might employ while struggling to win the superobjective *to reign*. Ristori consciously knew and articulated actions. She is one of the few actors in the twenty-five-hundred-year tradition of theater in the West before Stanislavski from whom we have such evidence, making it fair to assume that for all or most of that twenty-five hundred years the best actors have pursued their characters' inner actions intuitively.

In contrast, it is much more common to find actors on record speaking about "actions" but meaning what I call *activities.* For example, Leone DiSomi, an actor-manager in the second half of the sixteenth century—Shakespeare's era—tells us that "The actor . . . who learns his part well and has the requisite skill finds movements and gestures of an appropriate kind to make his part seem real. . . . [Thus] the actor has the business of keeping the variety of his actions appropriate to the situations."[31] DiSomi is clearly thinking about activity—behavior—rather than inner action. The seventeenth-century English actor Thomas Betterton is probably saying the same thing when he tells us that the actor "must adjust every action . . . [to] perfectly express the quality and manner of [his character]."[32] He refers to "action" but he does not speak with Ristori's clarity of purpose.

On the other hand, Sarah Kemble Siddons, in the eighteenth century, also speaking of Lady Macbeth, tells us that "She makes her very virtues the means of a taunt to her lord."[33] I take that to mean that Lady Macbeth uses her virtue *to taunt*, a sophisticated and interesting choice by another actress who speaks consciously of craft. Apart from rare artists like Ristori and Siddons, before the twentieth century it seems that there was only a dim intuitive realization by actors that they were pursuing "objectives" or "intentions"—inner actions. It is worth noting that Ristori and Siddons were women thinking with an analytical clarity at a time when few male theater persons seem to have done so. It was also a time when men were credited with having analytical minds and women were regarded as being entirely intuitive.

We have to credit Stanislavski with most carefully articulating and emphasizing the central importance of inner action that he called "the method of physical action." Some of his students were quick to pick up on his thinking, as Francis Fergusson tells us in an essay titled "The Notion of 'Action.'"[34] In the late 1920s, says Fergusson, Richard Boleslavsky and Maria Ouspenskaya "taught us that in finding the action of a character in a play, the only way to indicate it was by means of an infinitive. . . . Hence the action of *Three Sisters* is to get to Moscow."[35] Fergusson then goes on to ask if the concept of action is the same in Aristotle as it is for the Moscow Art Theater people, and he says,

> I am convinced that Boley and Madame were talking about the same thing Aristotle was: they too saw the movement of the psyche toward the object of its desire as what the dramatist was imitating in plot, character, and language, and what the actor imitates in the medium of his own feeling and perception. . . . *The Poetics* certainly makes more sense if one reads it after a long immersion in Boley's and Madame's practical lore of action.[36]

He is saying that theory makes more sense after engaging in the experiential process, an insight that applies to mastering the technique of inner action.

In *Acting: The First Six Lessons,* Richard Boleslavsky tells a young actress that her problem is a "lack of technique, that's all." "What technique?" she asks. And his reply is, "Of action's structure." "Stage action?" she asks, thinking, I suppose, of activity. "Dramatic action," he replies, "which the writer expresses in words, having that action as the purpose and goal of his words, and which the actor performs, or acts, as the word *actor* itself implies."[37] Boleslavsky is onto it, but he still doesn't make a clear-cut distinction between action and behavior when he says that the actor "acts" the action. Nevertheless, the need to clarify inner action is certainly what Boleslavsky is trying to get the young actress to understand. In *The First Six Lessons* Boleslavsky also asserts that *The Taming of the Shrew* is a play where two people "long to love."[38] When the young actress asks how the actor keeps performing that objective, Boleslavsky says, "I would make them remember it. I would ask them to have it behind every curse, every quarrel, every disagreement."[39]

Ben Kingsley put it this way: "What is our motivation, our objective, . . . our aim, . . . our intention? We use lots of words for the same thing. . . . If we had to reduce our modern tradition to one single point I think it would be this question."[40] In a conversation between Ian McKellen and John Barton, McKellen says, "Motivation is not a term that Shakespeare's actors would have understood. But the feeling behind what 'motivation' means . . . Shakespeare and his actors would have understood very well." And Barton replies, "Yes, they didn't have the word 'motivation' but Hamlet does talk about having 'the motive and the cue for passion.'"[41] Barton goes on to illustrate "the quality of a speech as opposed to the intentions behind it," and he strongly emphasizes the error in trying to perform moods or feelings and the necessity of doing intentions.[42] Later, when Barton is asked whether Shakespeare's words should be spoken "naturalistically" or in a "heightened" way, he says, "Let's ask ourselves our basic question, what's his intention?"[43] And the actress Sheila Hancock insists that you "first clarify your intention about why you're making the speech."[44] With respect to the matter of intention in a soliloquy, Barton says he thinks that the actor never speaks to himself, that he must speak to the audience because his intention is his need "to share his problems."[45]

If testimony were needed from eminent theater artists of the twentieth century who have validated Stanislavski's advice about inner action, look to Michel Saint-Denis, Jerzy Grotowski, Bertolt Brecht, Morris Carnovsky, Elia Kazan, Vakhtangov, and even Lee Strasberg. I've found the same testimony coming from eminent acting teachers like Robert Lewis, Stella Adler, Terry Schreiber, and Michael Kahn. The naysayers are few and their influence has been negligible, but even though the idea of objectives or intentions has been in the public arena since the 1920s, the technique of inner action remains obscure and undeveloped for many in our profession. Is there something subtle and elusive about the technique of inner action, something people, even now, are somehow hesitant to deal with? Do we really want to avoid knowing what we want to do?

The Actor's Task 6

*S*tanislavski emphasized the analysis and thorough understanding of

- the given circumstances in the script to fathom the facts presented as deeply as possible, and
- the flow of action in the scenes and those parts of the text that he called *bits* and that we have come to call *beats.*

Major figures in Western theater are on public record as agreeing with this analysis. Yet many still resist these simple, fundamental realities concerning the relationship of actor to text.

Why is this so? I see three reasons. First, until Stanislavski clearly articulated and emphasized his insight about the primacy of inner action late in the 1930s, few theater people over the centuries had shown any awareness of inner action or its basic importance. Second, there appears to have been a persistent confusion between the actor's perspective and the audience's perspective. The actor's inner craft creates an illusion that expresses what the audience sees: an authentic persona exhibiting exciting behavior and authentic feeling. That behavioral illusion is the blossom of the actor's craft. It is not the craft itself. The third reason for tardy recognition of inner action in our time is related to the vilification of Stanislavski's work during the 1970s and 1980s.

It is true that there is obscurity and confusion in Stanislavski's writings as they have come down to us. What we really have is a record of the evolution of his thought. It wasn't until he was infirm and close to death that he fully realized and stated the underlying importance of inner action. My prediction is that we will evolve Stanislavski's insight into techniques of inner action applicable to every genre of performance. The mastery of inner action is a robust creative force. As it becomes widely recognized, it will create a powerful impetus for the development of internal craft in all performers.

To many professionals today my analysis may be so laughably obvious, so fundamentally basic, that any serious discussion seems unnecessary. To others, the issues I have presented may seem to have a valid but not necessarily central place in the actor's work. To a few, any bother with inner action is a waste of time. All of that notwithstanding, there is no question in my mind that the flow of inner action as gleaned from a careful study of given circumstances is the core, the heart, and the most elemental part of the actor's relationship to text. I see seven basic principles governing the specifics of this relationship:

1. **The principal function of all the other skills of the actor's craft is to augment the ability to express the flow of inner action.** Mastery of that skill is at least the equal of if not fundamental to all other aspects of the actor's craft. Until the technique of inner action is mastered, the actor will never be able to understand or control fluctuations of performance from night to night. Furthermore, mastery of this technique leads not to a wooden consistency but to exploration of the actor's creative potential, enabling her to incarnate her unique version of the character in fresh and spontaneous performances. You have to know what the character wants to do in order to do it. The technique of inner action is required for the actor concerned with the interpretation of character.

2. **Skillful mastery of the technique of inner action *automatically* brings forth the expression of an authentic, complex, and spontaneous emotional expression from any performer willing to permit that expression.** This means that all of the energy and talk and misperception about developing techniques to generate *affect* has been a waste of time. The technique of inner action makes the expression of complex and appropriate emotion effortlessly

automatic. The correct affect will naturally follow. We will find the record filled with testimony to that fact.

3. **All performers on stage perform some kind of inner actions during every moment of performance.** Bad or mediocre performances—apart from problems of external technique—are those in which the performer consciously or unconsciously employs an inappropriate action. An actor's action rather than a character's action is inappropriate except for collaborative response. An actor must never go on stage wanting to impress his audience, "get it right," "do his best," "do a feeling," or pursue a personal aspiration. Our problem is that we tend to overlook the fact that all performances embody inner actions of some kind.

   A corollary to this observation is that an actor can perform only action. An actor cannot successfully go on stage and try to be something other than herself. Streep can only be Streep. She cannot be Sophie or anybody else. What she can do by articulating and pursuing the character's appropriate inner actions is incarnate the playwright's concept, and that's all. This simple fact gives the actor enormous possibilities. Streep can incarnate Hamlet. Her Hamlet will not be the Hamlet of everyone's expectations, but there is no reason why the maleness of the character should stand in her way. Actions, not genes or traits, define dramatic characters. Streep can play Hamlet just as Dustin Hoffman can play Tootsie. The trappings of external transformation merely enhance the expression of the character. Actions define character. Because Streep is a skilled actor, she can embody the character of Hamlet in her own unique way. All performers always perform a flow of inner action, so it is obvious that they should take control of the flow in harmony with the given circumstances.

4. **The technique of inner action will serve any theatrical style, genre, or form.** There is widespread testimony on the public record of this fact. It is a technique beyond style and basic to all styles. It will serve the purposes of American realism, British kitchen-sink naturalism, French Classicism, Restoration comedy of manners, Shakespeare, or Brecht. It will serve and respect the purposes of sixth-century Sanskrit drama, Beijing opera, Kabuki, Western classical ballet, and the works of Heiner Müller and Sam Shepard. Conscious articulation of inner action will serve the purposes of any performer, even those not creating a character. The widespread

belief that Stanislavski's insights are a matter restricted to realism should have been abandoned long ago.

5. **The use of the technique of inner action in rehearsal is a creative process enabling the actor and director to fathom the most profound possibilities in the script.** Probing the text with the technique of inner action opens it to the actor's deepest imaginative and creative potential. The technique is a tool that enables the actor to search out the fullest and most appropriate meaning of the words and subtext. Using inner action gives the actor precise control over the meaning of words.

   A corollary is that the playwright does not, in the end, give meaning to words. He hopes he has, but too often sees those hoped-for meanings missed. The director hopes she has given meaning to words, but unless she clearly articulated and communicated the flow of inner action to a concurring and skilled actor, the director will be disappointed. It is through conscious use of the technique of inner action that we most powerfully clarify and control the interpretation of text and give meaning to words.

6. **The technique of inner action is intimately related to the problem of achieving spontaneity in performance.** In addition to performing his character's inner actions, the actor must be prepared to respond spontaneously to his partners and environment, creating lively and slightly different performances while faithfully carrying out the wishes of the director. This process deepens the work of actors and requires them to accept the self totally and risk responses to their partners.

7. **Inner action differs from external activities—it is not gunfights, chases, kisses, handshakes, cigarette smoking, lovemaking, arguments, waving good-bye, hugs, or punches.** These are activities, not actions. An old theater term for some activities is *business.* Inner action governs, sometimes with the help of adverbs, how the activities or business are expressed.

We should also recognize that there is a problem associated with teaching and learning this technique. As human beings, most of us have an innate ability to act. Until our time most people, actors included, have believed that there is no sure technique to insure spontaneity and the expression of authentic feeling. The essence of the problem is that our innate acting ability, the intuitive knack, prompts many people to see the actor's work as almost mystical behavior beyond the bounds and possibilities of craft. Student actors who have had some intuitive successes and are infected with this fallacy may resist working to master the technique of inner action. Acting teachers, for perhaps the same reason, may come to the conclusion that it is a technique too peripheral to bother with. Directors may ignore it, thinking it entirely the responsibility of actors.

Like everything else in life, the technique of inner action is imperfect. There are negative outcomes if the individual actor blindly fights for his own inner actions without recognizing and responding spontaneously to the work of his partner. This mutual exchange requires an understanding of the dynamics of spontaneity and a willingness to risk. The relationship between playing the inner action and spontaneous behavior must be respected during both rehearsal and performance. But without a conscious technique of inner action, there are risks that are potentially more fatal than ignoring the technique:

- For the actor it will mean being at the mercy of that wild horse, talent. No matter how great personal talent, the mystery of why a performance was wonderful last night and dead tonight will plague the actor without the technique of inner action.
- When we ignore inner action, the possibility of misinterpretation increases. The technique provides a powerful tool for the exploration of creative possibilities emerging from the text. Because the actor gives meaning to words, it is in the interest of the playwright to make sure the actor knows what the characters want to do.
- When theater artists ignore inner action there will be negative consequences for the audience, especially the theatrically naive audience. Not only is it likely they will waste their time and money, they may begin to develop low standards of performance.

The actor's craft requires a mastery of both internal and external technique. My purpose has been to clarify an inner technique of incomparable power. Performers must learn to know and articulate the flow of inner actions. They have to develop the skill to play with and pursue those actions in a responsive way on stage. This inner technique is, finally, nothing more than the simple skill that vigorously animates every aspect of our lives: knowing the action we want to accomplish and working to achieve it.

The Role of the Audience 7

I f you go wide awake, healthy, and sober into a live performance after paying seventy dollars for a seat and then find yourself falling asleep halfway through act 1, it is not your fault. The actors have the responsibility to keep you awake. You have no reason to feel guilt, and there is no need to protect them from your boredom, frustration, and anger. If the performance is not working, if it is dull and soporific, the actors already know it. And I'll bet they were not consciously working with inner actions. In fact, they could probably feel the interaction between you dying. They could hear you snore. The sounds of snoring will only validate the actors' own experience. True, they will feel badly, but they can blame the problem on the playwright or the director if they want to deny their own responsibility.

Have you gone to see a dramatic play and experienced each new scene as real, but couldn't remember the preceding one? The scenes appeared authentic and emotionally valid but strangely forgettable. You are watching the second scene but don't recall what happened in the first one. Now that the third one is beginning, you've already forgotten the second. Like a string of pearls without the string, the performance doesn't hold together and has no shape. This is a common audience experience with a concrete explanation. The actors were playing moods instead of the inner action that holds the play together. We don't *follow* the action because there is no "action" to follow, only disconnected activity. There is nothing for us to track.

We track with actors playing actions because action focuses them, makes them intent. They are intent because they are struggling to achieve their intentions, their inner actions. They are focused because they want to do something! They make their struggle to achieve take place in front of us. We stay awake because pursuing an action or purpose is what living is about. We stay awake in the audience because we identify with that pursuit of purpose. We want to see if they'll make it, how they'll deal with the obstacles that confront them. In other words, we instinctively fulfill audience inner actions in response to the action on stage. The actors' actions provide a track for us to follow. They then engage us. They entertain.

There is a substantial misunderstanding of the word *entertain*. It doesn't mean happily jumping around to make people happy, which can be dreadful. To entertain is *to take in*. We expect actors to entertain, take in, and engage their audiences. That is their first task. Their second task is to keep the audience engaged without distraction until the final curtain falls.

Think about the difficulty of that assignment. What are human beings conditioned to do in darkened rooms? Sleep! The challenge actors take on is to keep us awake. Actors made a contract with us. For seventy dollars, they say they will keep us awake for two hours and send us from the theater aroused to laughter or tears. It's a contract audiences are willing to make every day. But how many times do we get our money's worth—even if we only pay a fraction of seventy dollars? And if we didn't get our money's worth, how many times have we meekly acted like we did? How many times have we loudly applauded a boring performance?

The American theater will rise again when audiences begin to demand their money's worth. Because we as audiences participate in theater, we have to do our part and demand the highest standard. Just as actors have a responsibility to respond spontaneously to each other, so do we have a responsibility to respond spontaneously to what they do on stage. Audiences who accept second-rate work help to create a second-rate theater—whether in their communities, their schools, or on Broadway. There is no need to be kindly. Actors look to audiences for validation and when we validate bad work, we lie. Living theater is too important for that.

I like to think that when actors come out for a curtain call, they come to present themselves for the audience's authentic response to their work. They come before the audience to take responsibility for their actions. They may deserve applause, but they may also deserve silence. But audiences seem to have lost that choice, believing they must always applaud. It is sad to have lost that choice. I think we will only have a truly exciting theater again if audiences regain that choice. It might not always be a polite or amicable response, but who decided that audiences had to be amicable? In the final analysis, what's wrong with honest?

It is time for theater to wake up and be renewed. It is time for audiences to demand high standards and thereby achieve their own most important inner actions: to condemn boredom and require the best.

Notes

1. In his essay "On Acting," Robert Benedetti makes a nice point about the Russian word often translated as "motivation" in Stanislavski's writing. Benedetti claims the word is more precisely translated as "aspiration" and that we must understand that motivation resides in the past while aspiration is directed at the future: "The proper sense of action, then, is a flow of energy from a motivating stimulus through a response directed toward an aspiration." The law and judicial system also distinguish between *intention* and *motivation*. According to the law, motivation resides entirely in the mind of a person. Intention, on the other hand, can be determined by behavior. If a person illegally carries a weapon, it can be inferred that his intention is to use it if he wishes. The presence of the weapon does not mean that he is motivated to cause injury by the weapon. His motivation would necessarily have to emerge from some other reason that, unless revealed, we cannot know.

2. Masaru Sekine in *Ze-Ami and His Theories of Noh Drama* quotes Ze-Ami as saying that Acting consists of the movements of an actor's body. If an actor moves his body, responding with his mind to the words and lines of a play . . . he will come to act naturally. . . . if he moves his head at the word *looking* in the text, if he points or withdraws his hand at the words *pointing* or *withdrawing*, and if he takes up a posture of listening at the word *listening*. What can a westerner reared on Western ideas make of this? Well, it really isn't very foreign. This is the way we train ballerinas, for instance. It seems to me that the most traditional way of training performers across the globe is to make them go through a rigorous discipline of learning specific movements and gestures to a

script or score so well that when they go on stage they do not have to think about their moves and their natural, confident, and unself-conscious being will do what has to be done in the best way possible. This is the Zen way proposed in *Zen and the Art of Archery*, and it is the method of Tadashi Suzuki. Sekine says as much when he tells us that "Ze-Ami's main point is that unconscious acting, acting from the Zen notion of nothingness or unself-consciousness is the ultimate ideal." The only difference with my argument here is that two different technologies for getting to that point have developed. I still prefer Stanislavski's approach because it balances the cognitive and the intuitive, requiring the actor to make an analysis of text and consciously articulate what the inner actions are. The Zen approach, like traditional ballet training, still eschews that element of inner work even though after diligent training and rehearsal everything in the end is deferred to the majesty of the self beyond self.

3. Hira Panth, "Bharatha's *Natyasastra* and Stanislavski's Acting Technique," 12.

4. Melissa Bruder et al., *A Practical Handbook for the Actor,* xi.

5. Jeffrey Sweet, *The Dramatist's Toolkit,* 2.

6. From a conversation in September 1992 with Anatoly Romashin, a well-known Russian actor, professor, and head of the acting program at the Moscow Institute of Cinematography. Romashin described the flow as a chain of actions, with each link in the chain loosely linked to those before and after. There is play between the links, enabling the actors to actually begin performing their next action as the previous action is being performed. This technique reinforces the conflict and interrelation of characters and their actions. I also see it as testimony to the Russian practice of dealing with the entire flow (or chain) of actions and not just the superobjective and a few subsidiary actions. Instructors in North America have to stop justifying their refusal to inculcate students with this necessary skill.

7. Following standard American practice, I use the word *beat* in this context. In Russia the term describing the smallest structural segment of a scene is *event.* Later in this text I use *event* in a very different way. There may come a time when people interested in the performing arts will define more precisely the terms we use and invent a common jargon, but I hope not. Our indifference to the usages of our colleagues probably serves to keep us more awake and thoughtful about the subtle differences at work in our barely disciplined discipline. I offer as an example my use of the term *event.*

Through my conversations with Anatoly Romashin and correspondence with Irina Levin (a coauthor of *Working on the Play and the Role*), I have come to see that we use the word *event* quite differently. For me the "event" in any scene is a pinpoint moment in time—usually toward the end of that scene—that tells us the outcome of the scene's struggle. This is a fairly common usage in the United States. This divergence between Russians and New Yorkers is interesting because the common American theatrical usage of *beat* began with a visit to Russia by some New York theater people in the 1920s who were advised by Stanislavski to work on a scene "bit by bit"—to work on the smallest pieces or segments of a scene (the *events* of Levin and Romashin). Listening to his Russian accent, Stanislavski's American visitors heard "beats" instead of "bits," and the word has stayed with us. Felicitously, *beat* suggests small structural elements as well as something about rhythm.

8. Bruce Weber, "Angels' Angels," 56.

9. Bernard Pomerance, *The Elephant Man,* 61. It is irrelevant to discuss whether my choices are right or wrong in any of these examples since there is no right or wrong in the business of interpretation. The only question that really matters is, Does it work? This is a complex question that must take into consideration several issues: Are all the choices I make consistent with the given circumstances? Do I honor the playwright's creation? Do my choices work for the audience? I think it is important when exploring the text in rehearsal that we be free to choose inner actions that would outrage conventional wisdom since this always leads to a deeper understanding of the textual possibilities and an enrichment of the performance.

10. Anton Chekhov, *The Seagull,* 349.

11. At this point I can hear some readers objecting that this process takes too much time. I really don't think this is the case. Even in summer theater in which an entire production is mounted in a week, the process can easily include consideration of the flow of action, even if outside of rehearsal time. Directors will find that actors who use the technique work faster than those who do not. The technique of inner action clearly facilitates the rehearsal process.

12. Robert Benedetti, "On Acting," 98.

13. Ibid., 97.

14. Stephen Nachmanovitch, *Free Play,* 42.

15. Daniel Goleman, "Happy or Sad, a Mood Can Prove Contagious," C1.

16. Ibid.

17. Ibid.

18. Ibid.

19. Nachmanovitch, "Mind at Play," 66–68.

20. Erica Munk, *Stanislavski and America,* 66.

21. Nachmanovitch, "Mind at Play," 89.

22. Mihaly Csikszentmihalyi, *Flow,* 36-42.

23. Found in Toby Cole and Helen Krick Chinoy's collection *Actors on Acting,* 13.

24. Ibid., 11.

25. Ibid., 14.

26. Ibid., 14.

27. William Archer, *Masks or Faces?,* 217.

28. Cole and Chinoy, *Actors on Acting,* 378.

29. Ibid., 354.

30. Ibid., 444.

31. Ibid., 48.

32. Ibid., 99.

33. Ibid., 143.

34. Francis Fergusson, "The Notion of 'Action,'" 85.

35. Ibid., 86.

36. Ibid.

37. Richard Boleslavsky, *Acting: The First Six Lessons,* 55.

38. Ibid., 56.

39. Ibid., 57.

40. John Barton, *Playing Shakespeare,* 9.

41. Ibid., 10-11.

42. Ibid.

43. Ibid., 16.

44. Ibid., 18.

45. Ibid., 102.

Bibliography

Adler, Stella. 1960. "The Art of Acting." *The Theatre* 2, no. 4 (April).
———. 1964. "The Reality of Doing." *Tulane Drama Review* 9, no. 1 (Fall).
———. 1988. *The Technique of Acting.* New York: Bantam.
Albright, H. D. 1947. *Working Up a Part.* Cambridge, MA: Houghton Mifflin.
Archer, William. [1888] 1957. "Masks or Faces." In *A Dramabook*, intro. by Lee Strasberg. New York: Hill and Wang.
Arnold, William. 1978. *Shadowland.* New York: McGraw-Hill.
Bakshy, Alexander. 1918. *The Path of the Modern Russian Stage.* Boston: John W. Luce and Co.
Barrymore, Ethel. 1955. *Memories.* New York: Harper and Brothers.
Barton, John. 1984. *Playing Shakespeare.* London: Methuen.
Belasco, David. 1919. *The Theatre Through Its Stage Door,* edited by Louis V. Defoe. New York: Harper and Brothers.
Benedetti, Jean. 1982. *Stanislavski: An Introduction.* New York: Theatre Arts Books.
———. 1988. *Stanislavski.* London: Methuen.
Benedetti, Robert L. 1970. *The Actor at Work.* Englewood Cliffs, NJ: Prentice Hall.
———. 1988. "On Acting." In *Master Teachers of Theater,* edited by Burnet M. Hobgood. Carbondale: Southern Illinois Press.
Bentley, Eric, ed. 1968. *The Theory of the Modern Stage.* Middlesex, England: Penguin Books.
Bernstein, Lester. 1975. "How the Actors Prepare at the Studio." *New York Times* 2 (February 2): 1, 13.
Black, Lendley C. 1987. *Michael Chekhov as Actor, Director, and Teacher.* Ann Arbor: University of Michigan Press.

Blanchard, Fred C. 1954. "Professional Theater Schools in the Early Twentieth Century." In *History of Speech Education in America,* edited by Karl R. Wallace. New York: Appleton-Century-Crofts.

Blum, Richard. 1984. *America in Film Acting: The Stanislavski Heritage.* Ann Arbor: University of Michigan Press.

Boleslavsky, Richard. 1933. *Acting: The First Six Lessons.* New York: Theatre Arts Books.

Boucicault, Dion. 1958. "The Art of Acting." In *Papers on Acting,* edited by Brander Matthews. New York: Hill and Wang.

Braun, Edward. 1969. *Meyerhold on Theater.* New York: Hill and Wang.

Bruder, Melissa, Lee Michael Cohn, Madeleine Olnek, Nathaniel Pollack, Robert Previto, and Scott Zeigler. 1986. *A Practical Handbook for the Actor.* New York: Vintage Books.

Calvert, Louis. 1918. *Problems of the Actor.* London: Simpkin, Marshall, Hamilton, Kent and Co.

Carnovsky, Morris. 1979. *The Theatre of Meyerhold.* London: Methuen.

———. 1984. *The Actor's Eye.* New York: Performing Arts Journal.

Chekhov, Anton. 1966. *The Seagull.* Translated by Stark Young. In *Twenty Best European Plays on the American Stage,* edited by John Gassner. New York: Crown Publishers.

Chekhov, Michael. 1953. *To the Actor.* New York: Harper and Row.

Clurman, Harold. 1935. "Conversation with Two Masters: From an Informal Diary of a Five Week Stay in the Soviet Union." *Theatre Arts Monthly* (November): 871–76.

———. 1945. *The Fervent Years.* New York: Alfred A. Knopf.

———. 1949. "Stanislavsky in America." *New Republic* 121 (August 22).

———. 1958. *Lies Like Truth.* New York: Grove Press.

Cohen, Robert. 1975. *Acting Professionally: Raw Facts About Careers in Acting.* Palo Alto, CA: Mayfield Publishing.

Cole, Toby, ed. 1955. *Acting: A Handbook of the Stanislavski Method.* New York: Crown Publishers.

Cole, Toby, and Helen Krich Chinoy, eds. 1970. *Actors on Acting.* New York: Crown Publishers.

Coquelin, Constant. 1958. "Art and the Actor." In *Papers on Acting,* edited by Brander Matthews. New York: Hill and Wang.

Csikszentmihalyi, Mihaly. 1990. *Flow: The Psychology of Optimal Experience.* New York: Harper and Row.

D'Angelo, Aristide. 1939. *The Actor Creates.* New York: Samuel French.

Diderot, Denis. [1778] 1957. *The Paradox of Acting.* In *A Dramabook,* intro. by Lee Strasberg. New York: Hill and Wang.

Duerr, Edwin. 1962. *The Length and Depth of Acting.* New York: Holt, Rinehart and Winston.

Easty, Edward D. 1966. *On Method Acting.* New York: House of Collectibles.

Edwards, Christine. 1965. *The Stanislavsky Heritage.* New York: New York University Press.

Fergusson, Francis. 1966. "The Notion of 'Action.'" In *Stanislavski and America: An Anthology from The Tulane Drama Review,* edited by Erika Munk. New York: Hill and Wang.

Filippov, Boris. 1977. *Actors Without Makeup.* Translated by Kathleen Cook. Moscow: Progress Publishers.

Funke, Lewis and John E. Booth. 1961. *Actors Talk About Acting: Fourteen Interviews with Stars of the Theater.* New York: Random House.

Garfield, David. 1984. *The Actor's Studio: A Player's Place.* New York: Collier Books.

Gielgud, John. 1937. "An Actor Prepares: A Comment on the Stanislavsky Method." *Theatre Arts Monthly* 21 (January).

Gilder, Rosamond. 1931. *Enter the Actress: The First Women in the Theater.* New York: Theatre Arts Books.

Goffman, Irving. 1959. *The Presentation of Self in Everyday Life.* Garden City, NY: Doubleday.

Goleman, Daniel. 1991. "Happy or Sad, a Mood Can Prove Contagious." *New York Times* (October 15): C1.

Gorchakov, Nikolai. 1954. *Stanislavsky Directs.* New York: Funk and Wagnalls.

Grotowski, Jerzy. 1968. *Toward a Poor Theater.* New York: Simon and Schuster.

Guthrie, Tyrone. 1957. "An Interview." *Equity* (December 9).

———. 1971. *Tyrone Guthrie on Acting.* New York: Viking Penguin.

Hagen, Uta. 1973. *Respect for Acting.* New York. Macmillan.

———. 1991. *A Challenge for the Actor.* New York: Macmillan.

Hart, Lynda. 1989. *Making a Spectacle.* Ann Arbor: University of Michigan Press.

Hayman, Ronald. 1969. *Techniques of Acting.* London: Methuen.

Herrigel, Eugen. 1953. *Zen in the Art of Archery.* New York: Pantheon Books.

Hethmon, Robert H., ed. *Strasberg at the Actors Studio.* New York: Viking Press.

Hewitt, Barnard, and Aristide D'Angelo. 1932. "The Stanislavsky System for Actors." *The Quarterly Journal of Speech* 17, no 3 (June).

Hill, John. [1746]. *The Actor.* London: R. Griffiths.

Hirsch, Foster. 1984. *A Method to Their Madness: The History of the Actor's Studio.* New York: W. W. Norton.

Hoffman, Theodore. 1960. "At the Grave of Stanislavsky." *Columbia University Forum* 3, no. 1 (winter): .

Joseph, Bertram. 1960. *Acting Shakespeare.* New York: Theatre Arts Books.

———. 1980. *A Shakespeare Workbook: Tragedies.* New York: Theatre Arts Books.

Kedrov, Mikhail. "The Last Experiment." In *Konstantin Stanislavsky: The Centennial Collection of Comments and Letters,* compiled by Sergei Melik-Zakharov and Shoel Bogatyrev, translated by Vic Schneierson.

Kristi, Grigori. 1973. "The Training of an Actor in the Stanislavski School of Acting." In *Stanislavski Today,* translated and edited by Sonia Moore. New York: American Center for Stanislavsky Theatre Art.

Levin, Irina, and Igor Levin. 1992. *Working on the Play and the Role.* Chicago: Ivan R. Dee.

Lewes, George H. nd. *On Actors and the Art of Acting.* New York: Grove Press.

Lewis, Robert. 1958. *Method or Madness?* New York: Samuel French.

———. 1980. *Advice to the Players.* New York: Harper and Row.

———. 1984. *Slings and Arrows: Theater in my Life.* New York: Stein and Day.

Logan, Joshua. 1949. "Rehearsal with Stanislavsky." *Vogue* 113, no. 10 (June).

McGaw, Charles. 1966. *Acting Is Believing: A Basic Method.* Second edition. Chicago: Holt, Rinehart and Winston.

Mackay, F. F. 1913. *The Art of Acting.* New York: F. Mackay.

Macleod, J. 1946. *Actors Cross the Volga.* London: Allen and Unwin, Ltd.

Magarshack, David. 1975. *Stanislavsky: A Life.* Westport, CT: Greenwood Press.

———. 1991. *Recycling Shakespeare.* New York: Applause Theatre Book Publishers.

Marowitz, Charles. 1964. *Stanislavsky and the Method.* New York: Citadel Press.

———. 1978. *The Act of Being: Toward a Theory of Acting.* New York: Taplinger Publishing.

Matthews, Brander, ed. 1958. *Papers on Acting.* New York: Hill and Wang.

Meisner, Sanford. 1964. "The Reality of Doing." *TDR* 9, no. 1 (fall): .

———. 1987. *On Acting.* New York: Vintage Books.

Meisner, Sanford, and Dennis Longwell. 1987. *Sanford Meisner on Acting.* New York: Vintage Books.

Mekler, Eva, ed. 1987. *The New Generation of Acting Teachers.* New York: Penguin Books.

Moore, Sonia. 1960. *The Stanislavski Method.* New York: Viking Press.

———. 1968. *Training an Actor: The Stanislavski System in Class.* New York: Viking Press.

Morris, Eric. 1988. *Acting from the Ultimate Consciousness.* Putnam, NY: Perigee Books.

Morris, Eric, and J. Hotchkis. 1977. *No Acting, Please.* Burbank, CA: Whitehouse, Spelling.

Munk, Erika, ed. 1966. *Stanislavski and America: An Anthology from the Tulane Drama Review.* New York: Hill and Wang.

Nachmanovitch, Stephen. 1990. *Free Play.* Los Angeles: Jeremy P. Tarcher.

Nemirovitch-Dantchenko, Vladimir. 1968. *My Life in the Russian Theatre.* Translated by John Cournos. New York: Theatre Arts Books.

Panth, Hira. 1992. "Bharatha's Natyasastra and Stanislavski's Acting Technique." Unpublished paper.

Pomerance, Bernard. 1979. *The Elephant Man.* New York: Grove Press.

Probst, Leonard. 1975. *Off Camera: Leveling About Themselves.* New York: Stein and Day.

Redgrave, Michael. 1953. *The Actor's Ways and Means.* London: Heinemann.

Ribot, Theodule. 1903. *The Psychology of the Emotions.* London: Walter Scott.

Roberts, J. W. 1981. *Richard Boleslavsky.* Ann Arbor, MI: UMI Research Press.

Ross, Lillian, and Helen Ross. 1962. *The Player: A Profile of an Art.* New York: Simon and Schuster.

Rutter, Carol. 1988. *Clamorous Voices: Shakespeare's Women Today.* London: Women's Press.

Saint-Denis, Michel. 1960. *Theatre: The Rediscovery of Style.* New York: Theatre Arts Books.

———. 1982. *Training for the Theatre.* New York: Theatre Arts Books.

Scher, Anthony. 1985. *Year of the King.* London: Methuen.

Schmidt, Willi. 1960. "The American Actor." *Equity* 45, no. 4 (April).

Schnitzler, Henry. 1954. "Truth or Consequences, or Stanislavsky Misinterpreted." *The Quarterly Journal of Speech* (April).

Sekine, Masaru. 1985. *Ze-Ami and His Theories of Noh Drama.* Gerrards Cross, England: Colin Smythe.

Selden, Samuel. 1947. *First Steps in Acting.* New York: F. S. Crofts and Co.

Shurtleff, Michael. 1978. *Audition.* New York: Walker and Co.

Siddons, Henry. [1822]. *Practical Illustrations of Rhetorical Gesture and Action Adapted to the English Drama.* London: Sherwood, Neely, and Jones.

Simonov, P. V. 1973. "The Method of K. S. Stanislavski and the Physiology of Emotion." In *Stanislavski Today,* translated and edited by Sonia Moore. New York: American Center for Stanislavsky Theatre Art.

Spolin, Viola. 1983. *Improvisation for the Theater.* Chicago: Northwestern University Press.

Stanislavsky, Konstantin. 1936. *An Actor Prepares.* Translated by E. R. Hapgood. NY, Theatre Arts Books.

———. 1948. *My Life in Art.* Translated by J. J. Robbins. New York: Theatre Arts Books.

———. 1958. *Stanislavski's Legacy.* Edited and translated by E. R. Hapgood. New York: Theatre Arts Books.

———. 1961. *Creating a Role.* Translated by E. R. Hapgood. NY: Theatre Arts Books.

———. 1986. *Building a Character.* Translated by E. R. Hapgood. London: Methuen.

Strasberg, Lee. 1987. *A Dream of Passion: The Development of the Method.* Edited by Evangeline Morphos. New York: Penguin Books.

Strickland, F. Cowles. 1956. *The Technique of Acting.* New York: McGraw-Hill.

Suzuki, Tadashi. 1986. *The Way of Acting.* Translated by J. Thomas Rimer, New York: Theatre Communications Group.

Sweet, Jeffrey. 1993. *The Dramatist's Toolkit.* Portsmouth, NH: Heinemann.

Talma. 1958. "Reflections on Action." In *Papers on Acting,* edited by B. Matthews. New York: Hill and Wang.

Warshow, Robert. 1974. *The Immediate Experience.* New York: Atheneum.

Weber, Bruce. 1993. "Angels' Angels." The New York Times Magazine (April 25).

West, Shearer. 1991. *The Image of the Actor.* New York: St. Martin's Press.

Wilson, Garff B. 1966. *A History of American Acting.* Bloomington: Indiana University Press.

Worthen, William B. 1984. *The Idea of the Actor.* Princeton, NJ: Princeton University Press.

Zakhava, B. E. 1955. "Principles of Directing." In *Acting: A Handbook of the Stanislavski Method,* compiled by Toby Cole. New York: Crown Publishers.